For Charlie, Toby and Freddie. May you stay out of trouble.

JAMES ACASTER'S CLASSIC SCRAPES

HEADLINE

First published in 2017
by HEADLINE PUBLISHING GROUP

5

Cataloguing in Publication Data is available from the British Library

Hardback ISBN 978 1 47224 718 6

Typeset in Sabon by Palimpsest Book Production Limited, Falkirk, Stirlingshire

Printed and bound in the UK by
CPI Group (UK) Ltd, Croydon CR0 4YY

Headline's policy is to use papers that are natural, renewable and
recyclable products and made from wood grown in sustainable forests.
The logging and manufacturing processes are expected to conform to the
environmental regulations of the country of origin.

HEADLINE PUBLISHING GROUP
An Hachette UK Company
Carmelite House
50 Victoria Embankment
London
EC4Y 0DZ

www.headline.co.uk
www.hachette.co.uk

ACKNOWLEDGEMENTS

When you're constantly messing up in life, the support and encouragement of the people around you is the only thing stopping you from giving up on your dreams. The following people have been amazingly supportive and hugely encouraging and I will always be grateful. A massive thank you to:

Josh Widdicombe, Neil Fearn, Charles Ballard, Richard Roper, Chris Lander, Amy Hopwood, Kate Watson, Georgia Jones, Phil McIntyre, David Acaster, Di Acaster, Stephen Acaster, Ruth Blythe, Amy Acaster, David Blythe, David Trent, Mick Trent, Graeme Wicks, Jake Ashton, Ben Foot, Josie Long, Milton Jones, Matthew Hill, Joe Steinhardt, Kate Foulds, Matt Ayre, Sam Holmes, Nish Kumar, Ed Gamble, Stuart Laws, Paul Bertellotti, Katie Philips, Tom Baxter, Rose Matafeo, Jim Watts, Katie Rock,

Tamsyn Payne, Joe Brown, Jack Barry, Lindsay Fenner, Nathaniel Metcalfe, Saurabh Kakkar, Josh Cole, Dan Lucchesi, Marina Veneziale, Reuben Humphries, Jim Hurren, Amanda Redman, Katherine Montgomery, Gary Keller, Ross Chudasama, Chris Hamilton, Rob Deering, Scott Blanks, Katie Cottrell, Cordelia Bradby, Trevor Lock, Alan Mason, Sid Harris, Ed Moore, Brett Goldstein, Joel Dommett, Stuart Goldsmith, Val Brownlee, Billy Brownlee, Alistair, Rybo, The King Fox and Mr Eko.

Foreword

by Josh Widdicombe

When I got a job on Saturday morning radio I mainly saw it as a chance to hang out with people I found funny and call it work. James Acaster was, and remains, the funniest person I know. There was never a grand plan that he would use this platform to tell me the story of his life disaster by disaster, and I have no idea how it evolved into that, but thank God it did, as I didn't have much else to fill the show with.

At some point James's stories became labelled Scrapes and then, I have no idea when, James became labelled the Scrapemaster. This had the added bonus of each week hearing the DJ of the show before mine – a man who clearly had no idea who James was or what his role on the show involved – having to read out what was coming up on my show: 'Josh has music from Pulp and Arctic Monkeys and will be joined by the Scrapemaster James Acaster.' The word 'Scrapemaster' was articulated with a mixture of confusion and disappointment for what clearly passes for radio entertainment these days.

At one story a week I presumed James would run dry after a few months but as you can see by the thickness of this book, I was very much mistaken. It was a peak era for James's scrapes. While he had many from his past (referred to on the show as 'archive Scrapes') they were still coming thick and fast in his life at this point. Being there when James told 'Failing to Tie a Tie' or 'Alastair' on the very week they had happened is the closest I will ever feel to being one of those people in the street watching The Beatles play on the roof of Abbey Road.

(I should say at this point that it sounds like I got a job on the radio and then just co-opted a funny friend to do the hard work for me for free. This isn't true, because as part of the deal I bought James 'a lunch of his choice' each week after the show. I remain thankful that James shares my love of mid-level high street restaurants and so the show was still viable financially.)

A lot of people described the Scrapes as like something out of a sitcom. However, I would say most of them are too far fetched for that – if you pitched half of them to a comedy producer they would be thrown out instantly: 'Holy Mackerel! No audience is going to buy this, it would never happen, this character is too weird!' But I can understand how all of them happened; whatever James's actions there is always a logic. I read a book recently that says the perfect sitcom plot should see the character acting logically to help themselves win, but actually making their situation worse with each action. This is the perfect description of James in the Scrapes. At each point I understand why he did what he did but never once does his decision making seem to do anything other than make things much, much worse. I understand and sympathise with every action within the Red Dress story but boy does he get himself into a sticky situation he doesn't need to be in.

Once the radio show ended I thought that would be the last I would hear of the Scrapes, apart from occasionally getting James to tell them in social situations, shouting out requests for the hits like I had gone to see the Kings of Leon. So I am delighted they have found a home in this book, a book which tells the tale of James's life in a way I hadn't expected. When James used to tell the stories on the radio show they would dot around his life with no real narrative week by week; it was James Acaster's life but reordered like the scenes in *Pulp Fiction*. Reading them chronologically it now feels like James has accidentally written his autobiography, the scrapes telling the story of the different stages of his life. Unlucky child, bored teenage drifter, eccentric musician, comedian. What all these periods have in common is that James had a lot of downtime and he didn't use it wisely. If James had gone to university or got a 9-5 job he wouldn't have had time to go to a porcelain exhibition or go dress shopping in Andover. It would have been easy to say he was wasting his youth, but it turns out he was sacrificing himself for his art like when George Orwell went to fight in the Spanish Civil war. Only funnier.

Now James is a successful comedian on our televisions he has less free time, and while I am delighted for him and his success I do worry this means the Scrapes will dry up. Please remember that each time you laugh at him on *Mock the Week* another Scrape has been averted. Still, maybe that is for the best. How much punishment can one man take? At points in this book James's life reads like the script for *Final Destination* – thank God he made it through in one piece.

Finally, I would also like to take this opportunity to say I was innocent of any involvement in cabadging James and I will be contacting my lawyers.

Hello

When I was a baby, I urinated into my own mouth. I don't remember doing it but my mother told me it happened and she has no reason to lie. As far as I can gather, I was lying on my back naked and somehow managed it. To be honest, I'd rather not go into details. The reason I'm telling you this is so that, straight out the gate, you know who I am and where I came from. This was how my life began and more or less how it continued for many, many years. This book is essentially the tale of a man repeatedly urinating into his own mouth. Pleased to meet you.

I should first of all point out that I never referred to these events as 'scrapes' until 2012 when my friend Josh Widdicombe got his own radio show and would invite me on each week to share a story with the listeners. I believe Josh began referring to them as 'scrapes' and it quickly stuck. I just think it's important that you know that I don't go around telling people that I get into lots of 'scrapes', as being seen as that kind of guy makes me feel uncomfortable.

I was very lucky to get the opportunity to tell these stories on Josh's show because I had tried telling them as part of my stand-up in the past and couldn't make them work. When I started out in comedy I had a very strict rule that everything I said on stage had to be true, and so I would tell these true stories without any embellishments and night after night the audience would still assume I was lying. Instead of getting laughs I'd be met with suspicion, scepticism and, on more than one occasion, silence. And so I started doing less autobiographical stand-up instead, which worked better for me but meant I had nowhere I could put these true stories.

Going on Josh's show every week was great because a radio environment is very different to that of a comedy club. It was much more like sitting around talking to my mates and so the stories were given a new lease of life. Obviously there will still be some people reading this book who will be sceptical, but that's fine, it's been really cool to finally find a home for all this material.

The reason why I'm more scrape-prone than most is hard to pin down. But I think the difference between me and someone who stays more or less scrape-free is a couple of seconds. In most of these stories if I'd just taken a couple more seconds to consider my options I would've been fine. But instead I went with the first idea that popped into my head and ended up with a mouthful of urine.

I think it's best that I start from the earliest scrape I can remember and just carry on from there. The first scrape anyone ever gets themselves into is quite unique, because they've never been in this sort of situation before (as far as they can recall) and so everything that happens introduces them to emotions they never knew they had. However, unlike most people, I don't get any better at dealing with these emotions as my life progresses. If you compare the first story in this book to the final story you'll see that they essentially happen to exactly the same person, a person who has learned absolutely nothing throughout his entire life. This first story takes place when he is five and as wise as he's ever going to be.

Towel

I didn't realise this was unusual at the time, but I went to a primary school that didn't have any hand driers or paper towels so the students had to bring in their own towels every day from home.

Even after changing to a different primary school that did not have this rule, I still thought there was nothing out of the ordinary about having to bring a towel into school every day until I was in my twenties and, whilst chatting to a group of people at a party, said, 'Yeah, it's like when you were a little kid and you used to have to bring your towel into school with you!' As everyone stared back at me blankly it dawned on me that this might not be the universal experience I once thought it was. But between the ages of five and six I would walk to school carrying a rolled-up towel under my arm and saw nothing wrong with that whatsoever.

James Acaster on his way to school aged 5

This is the story of the day I forgot my towel. This is also the story of the first time I ever got in trouble. Let's face it, the two usually go hand in hand. Anyone who has ever needed a towel but has failed to bring said towel usually ends up in some form of trouble. They've opened themselves up to all sorts of issues, probably the kind that concern how wet or dry something or someone is going to be at any given moment during the day. I should point out that I did not get told off for forgetting my towel. I could've handled that. Receiving a swift but stern lecture about how I need to remember to bring my towel into school and how I have to learn to be responsible – that would have been fine and may have even made me a better person in the long run. But I didn't realise I'd forgotten my towel until it was too late.

I'd been to the toilet, washed my hands properly with soap and warm water, then stepped from the toilets into the cloak room where my towel should have been and realised I'd left it at home. I froze, soapy water dripping from my hands. I had never made a mistake like this before in my entire life. I don't know if you remember the first time you ever forgot to do something but it feels completely surreal. You've got no frame of reference for it, you've literally never experienced this level of panic before, and there's no one around to help you. I was on my own, no adults to turn to for help. I couldn't walk into the classroom with soapy hands and ask the teacher to help me, I'd be an instant target for bullies – plus I could have got into trouble for dripping soapy water on to the classroom floor and at this point I had an immaculate behaviour record that I didn't fancy marring just because I couldn't handle my own business.

There was one other kid in the cloakroom, whose name was Simon. All I remember about Simon is that he had very straight hair and a very posh voice. That's it. He was sitting on a bench tying his shoes up.

Here's what I could've said: 'Simon, can I borrow your towel?' Looking back now as a thirty-two-year-old I think that would've been my best bet, because if Simon had said yes, I could've dried my hands on his towel and then continued with my day. But I didn't ask Simon if I could borrow his towel. Instead I said, 'Who in our class do you hate the most?'

He gave it some consideration then answered, 'Siobhan.'

So, as a favour to Simon (I assume), I walked over to Siobhan's coat, which was hanging up on her coat hook, and proceeded to dry my hands on her coat. Perhaps the reason why I asked Simon who he hated the most was so Simon and I would be in this together, as technically this had now been his idea as well. If I had just dried my hands on the coat of the person I, James Acaster, hated the most then I would be solely to blame, whereas now I had someone I could take down with me if things turned sour.

And yet I don't think that was the reason I asked Simon who in our class he hated the most. Because, the truth is, it never occurred to me that I would get caught or get into trouble for this. I had never been in trouble before, the concept of 'getting caught' was completely foreign to me. As far as I was concerned, Siobhan's coat would be dry by the time she came to put it on at the end of the school day and no one would ever know what I'd done, it'd just be a secret between Simon and I. I think the real reason I asked Simon who he hated the most was because I had found myself in a pickle and decided that I *had* to wipe my hands on a classmate's coat and since I felt bad about this, I tried to turn this bad deed into a good deed for someone else. And so I asked Simon who he hated the most, then used his enemy's coat as a towel as a little treat for Simon. Plus I would be wiping my hands on a bad person's coat (because surely no one would ever hate a good person) and therefore not really being that naughty myself. If you do a bad thing to a bad person then that makes you a good person, doesn't it? Everybody knows that.

As five-year-olds go, Siobhan was in fact a very good person. She never did anything wrong to anyone and did not deserve having her coat used as a hand towel by a forgetful classmate. After this incident we actually became friends, and one day when she opened her lunchbox to discover her chocolate bar was missing, we launched a full investigation between the two of us and unearthed the culprit (a boy named Anthony. NOT Simon. Although he was our initial suspect for obvious reasons). If you happened to see us that day, working together like proper detectives, you would never guess that just a few months previously we had been on opposite sides of the fence.

After wiping my hands on a little girl's coat, I went about my day and forgot all about what I'd done because, as I said, I had never been in trouble before and so did not think that I would get caught because I simply didn't know what that even was. I was in a great mood that day because as far as I was concerned, I had solved a problem using my head. Very proud of myself. Very proud, indeed.

Then afternoon registration rolled around and Mrs Andrews had an announcement to make. Siobhan was very upset, and the reason she was upset was because someone had left big soapy streak marks all over her new coat. Inside my five-year-old brain, all hell broke loose. I didn't know soap left streak marks!!! I had no idea there would be even a shred of evidence left behind!!! This was meant to be the perfect crime!!! I then felt a feeling way worse than the dread I had felt when I realised I'd forgotten my towel. For the first time in my life I felt a crushing sense of guilt. Guilt and fear, actually. I'd felt fear before, obviously. I was five and ever since I'd started school I'd been afraid of everyone and everything, but this was way more intense. Until then I'd only feared things that I didn't deserve, like death or the TV breaking, but this was the first time that I was feeling fear because of something I had brought on myself, and that if something bad happened to me as a result no one would give me any sympathy because I one hundred per cent had it coming.

I couldn't quite believe what was happening. It felt like a dream. And then I saw, in slow motion, Simon raising his hand, his hair all straight on his head, and telling Mrs Andrews, in his posh little voice, 'It was James Acaster.'

My whole world was falling apart.

I couldn't believe he would turn on me like this – I only chose Siobhan because he said he hated her! Mrs Andrews told me off in front of the whole class. 'You should know better' were the words I still remember to this day. Over and over: 'You should know better'. If I was articulate enough I would've told her that I was five and so of course I did not know better. The only reason I had been caught was because I *didn't* know better. Why would a five year old who has never been in trouble or done anything naughty in his whole life know better than anyone about anything at all? The only person who should know better in this room, Mrs Andrews, is you! If we caught you wiping your hands on all of our coats then it would be acceptable to say, 'Mrs Andrews. You, a woman in your fifties, should unquestionably know better.' But I have only existed for five years. So if you want to tell me off you should say, 'James Acaster, because you do not know how the world works, you have understandably made a huge mistake. I'm now going to punish you for it so you don't do it again. If you do do it again I will tell you that you should know better. But this time, you did not and that was your undoing.'

As everyone got up from the floor and sat down at their desks for the start of the lesson, I turned to Simon and said, 'But you said she was your least favourite person in the whole class.' Simon smiled, put his bag over his shoulder and replied, 'Second least favourite.'

Juggling

Fast-forward a couple of years and not only am I not getting in trouble in school any more but I've also got a buzzing social life due to joining the Cubs. The Cubs is Scouts for seven- to ten-year-olds. Before the Cubs I was in the Beavers and then after Cubs went on to become a Scout. I am not sure why it happens in this order. In the wild a beaver does not become a cub and a cub does not become a scout. They are all different species. Also, a beaver would be older than a cub in the wild. Unless it's a baby beaver, but a baby beaver should strictly be referred to as a kitten. Obviously, I understand how it would be confusing to rename the Beavers 'the Kittens', because then everyone would think about cat babies. Even if you changed the Beavers to 'the Beaver Kittens', not everyone would feel comfortable with it. I just think the Scouts should pick a species and follow it through logically. I vote to replace the name Beavers with 'Cubs' then change Cubs to 'Tigers' and Scouts to 'Older Tigers'. This would be a better name for the Scouts because, like tigers, the number of Scouts is rapidly depleting and the common Boy Scout is on the verge of extinction. Bear Grylls is doing everything he can to keep those knot-tying pipsqueaks alive but maybe all they really need to do is update the brand and then numbers would pick up. The same goes for actual tigers. If tigers changed their name to Stripy Lions then we'd all be interested anew.

Every now and then, my Cub Pack would put on a performance for the mums and dads. The performance would usually be themed and involve singing, maybe some dancing, and whatever skills the Cubs had up their sleeves (imagine how much cooler this story would be if I was saying 'Tigers' instead of Cubs right now. Imagine how much cooler still this story would be if I was saying 'Stripy Lions' instead of Tigers). The only performance I remember taking part in was the circus-themed show we did in my first year. We would be performing in a small room to about forty parents, and each one of us had to perform a different circus skill. I wanted to be a clown (naturally) but the clown roles got snapped up pretty quickly. In fact, all the good parts were going pretty fast. I think it was for this reason that I lied and said I could do something I couldn't do, just so I got a decent part in the show.

'Who can juggle?' asked Akela (named after the wolf in *The Jungle Book* just to further confuse anyone trying to figure out what the theme is here. All the leaders were named after *Jungle Book* characters but why I just don't know. The theme of the

Cubs is as confused as whatever theme Alton Towers thinks it's selling these days. They both appear to go for a bit of everything and hope something sticks and if they weren't so much damn fun to go to then they'd definitely get taken to task for it). When Akela asked who could juggle, two hands went up: a boy called Matthew who had learned to juggle at an after school club, and a boy called James Acaster who didn't know what juggling was.

Since nobody else raised their hand, both Matthew and I were chosen to be the jugglers.

It had been a big year for me in terms of live performance. Just a couple of months previous I had landed the lead role in the St Andrew's Primary School Christmas play, *The Woodcutter and the Christmas Dove*. I played a little character known as The Woodcutter. Calling it a big deal would be downplaying it. The previous year I had played a schoolboy (which isn't acting when you are also a schoolboy in real life) and had one line during the first two minutes of the play before never being seen again (the line in question was, 'He could even wear glasses' when talking about a sheepdog.) Now I was THE Woodcutter in a play that I assumed was known to the entire world as a true classic. The Christmas Dove (played by promising newcomer Jenny Cottrell) was on a mission to deliver the good news of Jesus' birth to another character in the play (I forget who) but tragically got injured outside the woodcutter's house (I forget how). Being a wonderful man, the woodcutter nurses the dove back to health so it can fly again and as a result bags himself an invite to the birth of the one true Christ but annoyingly fails to get a shout out in the Bible.

I was not prepared for a solo. As in singing on my own. The

melody of 'A Woodcutter's Prayer' still haunts me to this day. Usually when I'm about to go to sleep I hear the refrain 'A crib full of emptiness, a woodcutter's prayer' faintly, as if drifting ghostlike across the moorland of my troubled mind. I bottled it. In rehearsal I literally could not make audible sound come out of my mouth every time I was supposed to sing that depressing, high-pitched song about how the woodcutter was unable to have kids and so will give all his love to a dove he found half-dead on the floor. On the day of the performance the teacher directing the play decided that the song would become a group number and even then I opted to mime along while standing centre stage holding a tiny plastic axe in one hand and a toy dove in the other. I am convinced that my appalling interpretation of the character of The Woodcutter is the main reason I have never seen another production of *The Woodcutter and the Christmas Dove* advertised anywhere else since. It was my one shot and I blew it.

This meant I was even more determined *not* to blow it a second time at the Cub Scout Circus Show. I had chosen to be a juggler mainly because they didn't have to do any singing, but had overlooked the fact that I had never juggled before. So I did what any boy who's bitten off more than he can chew does and I went home and I asked my father for help. 'Dad, can you juggle?' I asked, and he confidently replied, 'Yes. Yes I can!' Because as it turns out, I'm not the only liar in the family.

The next morning I went out and bought a set of juggling balls with my pocket money and took them home to my father. He opened the box, looked at the three balls inside, picked one up and announced, 'Right, we don't need this one,' and threw it over his shoulder. Alarm bells should've started to ring at this point but I was seven years old and this man was the wisest person I'd ever met so I assumed he knew what he was doing. That was clearly just the spare ball. Which makes total sense – I'm going to be throwing these balls all over the place, it's only a matter of time before I lose one of them and so a spare ball is almost certainly essential. And then the lesson began. Now, you may not know how to juggle. Maybe you've seen other people juggle but never given it a go yourself. So just in case you were thinking about taking it up, here is the technique my father taught me all those years ago:

Step 1 - Stand up straight with a juggling ball in each hand.

Step 2 - Throw the ball in your left hand high into the air.

Step 3 - While the first ball is in the air, *PASS* the second ball from your right hand to your left hand. Do not *throw* the ball – *PASS* THE BALL.

Step 4 - Catch the falling ball in your right hand.

Step 5 - Repeat steps 2 to 4. You are now a professional juggler.

In less than a minute I had mastered this technique. I was standing in front of the mirror, throwing and passing on a loop, and once I had been doing this for two minutes my father raised his hands nonchalantly and said, 'And that's juggling.' End of lesson.

I had learned to juggle in no less than two minutes, so I was sure to nail the Cub Scout Circus show. If I'm honest, though, I did have *some* doubts – the way I juggled didn't look the same as the juggling I'd seen other people do. But my dad seemed 100 per cent sure that what I had done was identical to, if not better than, any juggling I had ever seen, and there was no way this man would send me into any situation without every tool I needed to ensure my success.

The night of the big show came around and the Cubs were gathered backstage (by backstage I mean another room in the church building we had our Cub meetings in), all of us dressed in our various circus costumes. I was sitting on the floor holding my two juggling balls, wearing a shirt, school trousers and a waistcoat, because I was a juggler and that's what jugglers wear. Matthew was wearing the same outfit as me but I noticed he was carrying *three* juggling balls and not two. I couldn't believe it. What an idiot! He'd brought the spare ball along! Oh boy! Best of luck, Matthew! Honestly, what a wally, he's about to humiliate himself in front of all the mums and dads. Oh Matthew, you poor, poor Cub Scout, Baden Powell would be spinning in his grave.

It was showtime. Akela (the Cub leader, an adult) was the first onstage (the patch of floor in front of where the parents were sitting). She welcomed the audience to the big top (drafty church room) and introduced the acts one by one. The clowns came out and did an amusing routine where they pushed each other over and laughed silently; there was a kid dressed as a lion tamer and another kid dressed as a lion whose chair act went down a dream; one kid was a tightrope walker but instead of a tightrope he walked along a rather wide bench – what an amateur.

'And now!' announced Akela in a big booming voice, 'it's time for... the JUGG-ER-LORS!!!!' Matthew and I marched onstage and stood right at the front, me on the left and him on the right and then we began to juggle. In our own individual ways. I launched into my honed routine with ease – throw, pass, catch, throw, pass, catch, throw, pass, catch, throw, pass, catch – never dropping a single ball, standing up nice and straight throughout. The parents, however, didn't appreciate what they were seeing. They looked sort of amused but hardly impressed. Then more and more of the parents started looking over at Matthew; in fact, pretty soon all the mums and dads were looking over at Matthew, and I presumed he must be making such a pig's ear of things, what with bringing the spare ball along and all, that they were all watching him out of morbid curiosity. I decided to look over myself. It felt cruel but I had to see what kind of mess he'd got himself into.

In my memory he was the best juggler the world has ever seen. Passing balls underneath his legs while he did high kicks, his arms weaving over and under each other like an octopus, doing that trick where you catch the balls from the top rather than the bottom and drop them so it looks like you're juggling upside down. I think he was even shouting 'Woo!' every so often to get the crowd hyped up even more. It was at this point that I began to suspect I was not a juggler and that, although what I was doing may be technically considered juggling by a tiny minority of the world's population, in this church hall alongside a boy who may have legitimately run away with the circus, it was nothing more than moving two balls from one hand to the other without dropping them on the floor.

Matthew did his big finale, all three balls thrown high into the air at once then incorporating the triple catch with a bow, and the crowd went wild and crazy. There were cheers and stamping of feet, whistling too, and then the kid who was dressed as a lion jumped out from behind a cardboard cannon and pointed at Matthew with two hands just in case the parents weren't 100 per cent clear on which juggler they were applauding.

A Lion Cub

I looked out at the parents all losing their minds over Matthew and saw only one person looking at me – my dad, standing at the back, looking extremely proud and giving me a solid thumbs up.

Eureka!

I want you to know that my father was a much better dad than that juggling story made out. Not that the previous story even shows him in a particularly bad light; upon reflection he helped me out as best he could and tried to give me the confidence I needed approaching an impossible situation that I alone had gotten myself into.

When I was eight my father made a deal with me that if I saved up twenty pounds he would make up the difference so I could buy a cymbal for my drum kit. A lot of details in that sentence point to him being a cool dad. For starters he had let me not only learn the drums but also have a drum kit in the house. He had also paid for me to have drum lessons instead of teaching me himself as there was no way I was going to let *him* teach me for fear he had me lightly pat the drums with my palms and make drum noises with my mouth before raising his hands nonchalantly and saying, 'And that's drumming.' Also, making this deal with me was a great idea because back then I found it impossible to save up my pocket money and would instead spend every penny exclusively on sweets, and if it wasn't for my father making this deal with me I'd probably be spending my entire annual income on pick 'n' mix to this day.

During this time the family visited Eureka!, an interactive science museum for kids, in Halifax. Before I continue this story, may I just say that Eureka! is a fantastic place and a wonderful day out for children of all ages. I myself had an amazing time there, until the very last minute when my life turned to shit.

I don't know if this is still a feature at Eureka! these days but during my visit there was a section of the museum all about the workplace and how science plays a role in different working environments. In the 'science in the workplace' section of Eureka! there was an assembly line to demonstrate how machinery works and how the things we take for granted in everyday life are made. When I say assembly line, it was really a small collection of simple machines that, if used in the correct order, could make a basic Styrofoam lunchbox. And it was up to us kids to make these lunchboxes. There were four machines: the first one cut out the two halves of the lunchbox, the second one made the holes for the hinges and handle, the third put the hinges on the lunchbox and the fourth put the handle on it. Kids would go into the room in groups of four and work the machines for ten minutes, and by the end they would understand a little more about how machines work, a little bit more about what it's like to have a job, and possess a lunchbox that would fall apart in the car on the way home.

My brother, sister and I went in together along with some kid we'd never met before and sat at the machines. A Eureka! employee entered the room to welcome us to work and explain how all the machines operated, and then they sounded some sort of foghorn signifying the start of the working day. We started to work slowly, making the Styrofoam lunchboxes, one step at a time. I worked on the machine that put the hinges on the lunchbox, in my opinion the worst machine of the four. Cutting out the two halves looked fun, the second machine was basically a giant hole-punch and the fourth machine gave you the finished product. Putting on the hinges was D-U-L-L. I was just eight years old and here I was, pulling a lever which would put the boring hinges on to the boring lunchbox. Man alive. My sister was loving working on the giant hole-punch machine. You could see the satisfaction in her eyes every time she pulled that lever; she was so lucky. I loved hole-punches as a child but never had cause to use them. The amount of children doing their own filing is startlingly low. I often think it's a shame that hole-punches are so much fun but are seldom used by the people who'd appreciate them the most. Hole-punches, much like swivel chairs, are wasted on adults. A child looks at your average office and sees a playground; an adult looks at an office and sees a prison sentence. Then there are adults who love swivel chairs and hole-punches but can't openly enjoy them because they aren't children any more and their playground days are over. The universe is cruel.

At the end of our shift they sounded the foghorn again then, to our surprise, handed out payslips for twenty pounds. Twenty pounds – the exact amount of money I needed to save up in order to get a cymbal for my drum kit. There is a God.

'Here's your pay for the day!' said the Eureka! staff member cheerily. 'Take these down to the cash machine next to the main entrance and you will be given your wages!'

All the kids got excited except for me. I wasn't going to celebrate just yet. Unlike these other punks, I really needed this money. But even at the age of eight I knew that nothing in life comes this easy. I stayed behind after my co-workers had left the room to ask the boss a question.

'This isn't real money is it?' I double checked, pretty sure that Eureka! weren't actually going to pay us all twenty pounds each for *real*. He looked surprised.

'Why yes it is!' he said. 'That's your pay for the day! It's real all right! Good work, little buddy!'

I hesitated for a second. Then, and this moment still makes me cringe as an adult, with him watching me, I jumped, twirled in mid-air and shouted in a high-pitched voice, 'Eureka!'

Then I skipped out of the room, got into the lift with my family and practically danced as the lift moved down through the floors, imagining how great that new cymbal was going to sound on my drum kit. We reached the ground floor and I strutted out of the lift ahead of everyone else, straight on up to the Eureka! cash machine, where I put my payslip in the slot and then out came... *Eureka! money*. A note with goddamn Archimedes' idiot face on the front and the stupid number '20' written next to him in a bullshit childish font. As an adult it occurs to me that you may be able to spend that money in the Eureka! gift shop, perhaps to purchase stationery or maybe even a T-shirt. There were fun science-y toys on sale too; maybe I could've bought one of those. But I'll never know because I immediately tore the money up, threw my lunchbox in the bin and sulked in the car all the way home. And with that, my lesson about how it feels to have a day job was well and truly learnt.

Jobs

Maybe it's because of Eureka! that I've never truly excelled in the workplace. Before comedy I had many different jobs. My first was at Kettering's own theme park, Wicksteed Park, home of the Pinfari roller coaster. If you ever meet someone from Kettering who describes Kettering as a 'shit hole', remember that the shit hole they're talking about has a roller coaster in it, so maybe it's not as bad as they're making out. At Wicksteed, my job was to sell food and drinks, mainly ice cream and ice blasts, from an outlet called The Oak Tree (the natural home of all things ice).

On my first day there my co-worker, Cetin, who was giving me the tour said, 'This is the hot drinks machine. You can make tea, coffee, hot chocolate, but if the hot chocolate runs out, you've got to change the bag of hot chocolate powder in the machine, and once, yeah, I opened a new bag of hot chocolate powder and a cloud of hot chocolate powder poofed up in my face and later on that day I sneezed and it tasted like hot chocolate.'

I knew in that moment that I couldn't work in The Oak Tree. He was a lovely man, but if that was his best anecdote since working at the park then I was terrified, terrified to my very core. I didn't want to end up telling people what my sneezes tasted like, even if they did taste like hot chocolate. Oh, and by the way, it didn't taste like hot chocolate did it? It tasted like chocolate. Nothing tastes like *hot* chocolate. Something can taste like chocolate but not *hot* chocolate. Hot chocolate is not a flavour. It's a temperature that a flavour can be served at but it's not its own flavour. Hot chocolate tastes like chocolate, the only thing that makes it taste like hot chocolate is the fact that it's hot, so unless Cetin did a hot sneeze then his sneeze tasted like normal chocolate. These were the thoughts that went through my head during my very first shift.

After Wicksteed I taught the drums in a music shop. I had so many students, of which about three ever actually practised the drums outside of their lessons. One child, a seven-year-old who was also called James, would turn up every week with a new excuse as to why he hadn't practised. One week he told me, 'I wasn't able to play the drums this week because I've really been getting into writing down car number plates.' It was hard to be angry with him. Whether he's telling the truth or lying, what a brilliant mind. I hope he was being honest and that he really did spend a week walking the streets making a note of any car number plate that tickled his fancy. I never found out if he was only writing down the number plates of cars he thought looked suspicious or the number plates of cars he thought looked cool and therefore might want to buy one day when he's an adult. There's every chance he was just writing down every single car number plate for no reason other than to do it, like a train spotter but with cars. Maybe he'd take them home and read them and find hidden messages in them like in *A Beautiful Mind*. With any luck one of the hidden messages would've been, 'Stop writing down car number plates and do some effing drum practice, mate.'

After drum teaching I worked in a pub kitchen for three years. It was a family pub and I think it's best I don't say the name of it, but it was also in Kettering. It was the kind of kitchen where many pranks took place, great hilarious pranks such as pulling people's trousers down, throwing jacket potatoes at people's nuts, throwing steak knives at people's feet, putting the metal tongs on the grill until they heat up then hanging them up again and asking someone to flip one of the steaks over with them, putting Tabasco on someone's straw in their glass of water, getting someone's personal belongings from the changing rooms then wrapping them in cling film then putting them in a bucket of haddocks in water so that by the end of the shift they smell like rank fish. Oh the laughs we had.

Sometimes pranks would go awry. One afternoon when the pub was pretty quiet, only fifteen or so customers scattered around eating food, the manager was talking to one of the chefs out in the main dining area. She was saying how impressed she had been with his attitude since working at the pub, how well he had done and that if he kept going the way he's going, a promotion might be in order. At this point a wacky waiter decided to prank the chef. He had assessed the situation and decided that since none of the customers were looking over in their direction it was fine to pull the chef's trousers down. And that's exactly what he did. In front of the manager. Also, the chef wasn't wearing any pants that day. So he was now naked from the waist down and, I'm told, had quite the dong. Obviously, this was extremely embarrassing for the chef who immediately saw red, turned round and started beating up the waiter in front of the customers, dong still fully on display and swinging around all over the shop, with the waiter fully crying while the beating was taking place. Neither employee was fired.[1]

It was a joyous place to work and yet I still decided to leave. As I said, I had been there for three years, and on my final day a waitress was also leaving. She had been there for just over six months and left with armfuls of presents and cards from the waiting staff and bar staff, people she now considered to be her friends. There were so many presents, in fact, that they had to help her lift them all into the car. The kitchen staff I worked with favoured a slightly different approach when it came to goodbyes. When my shift ended at eleven p.m. I walked to my car and saw that they had covered it in dessert sauce and haddock water. There was caramel and chocolate sauce all over the car – they had even put the sauce under the door handles, making it impossible to get into the car and access my cleaning products

---

1 I wasn't actually present when this took place; it was told to me by the kitchen staff and to be fair there were a lot of liars who worked at this particular pub. However, either way I love it and the fact that I believe it, even if it didn't happen, lets you know exactly what kind of a place this was to work in.

(this touch was genius, to be fair). An entire bucket of haddock-y juices had been dumped on the roof, coating the body of the car and getting into the air vents, meaning the inside of the car would never stop smelling of fish ever again. Obviously I went back inside and got the names of the perpetrators from the bar staff. One of them didn't answer his phone and the other was furious when I asked him to come back and clean the car.

He reluctantly returned, and while scrubbing the bonnet he moaned at me, 'I mean, what makes you think I want to be cleaning your car at eleven thirty at night?' to which I replied, 'What made you think that *I* want to be cleaning my car at eleven thirty at night?' Maybe I had misread the entire situation and this had been a gesture of love all along? 'It's James's last day, we all know what he's into, little treat – late night car wash! Don't forget he can't get enough dessert sauce and he loves retching every time he breathes in so do not skimp on the haddock! Farewell, Acaster, good luck in all your future endeavours!'

I have since learned an extra detail about this event that makes me understand why the guy who came back was so angry. There were actually three people who dessert-bombed my car that night. The third one was an actual friend of mine who also worked in the kitchen and had somehow got out of being named by the staff at the bar. It's understandable that the person who ended up cleaning the car with me would be angry because really the worst of the bunch was this so-called friend of mine; he was the one who truly betrayed me after all. In fact, the friend in question still doesn't know that I know as we've never talked about it. So, just in case he's reading this – fuck you, Olly.

Assembly

I seem to have leapt straight from primary school to part-time employment, which is poor form on my part. To do so would be to miss out secondary school, the most embarrassing years of anybody's life. Secondary school is a minefield of humiliation and your first year there is particularly tricky. A single event during that first year can shape how your classmates view you for the next five. It can mould who you are as a human being, especially if it takes place in front of literally everybody else in your entire school year at exactly the same time.

Every Monday a different year seven form group would put on an assembly for the rest of the year sevens. Most of the time the assemblies were about a serious subject and were informative and you'd just switch off for the whole thing while kids took it in turns to read facts from pieces of paper. Then one Monday, one form group changed assemblies for ever. Mr Martin's class knocked it out the park; they pulled out all the stops and put on their very own version of *Shooting Stars*. That was it: they didn't try and teach us anything, they just wrote an amazingly funny assembly. To this day it's probably the greatest live performance I have ever seen.

Two kids called Danny and Craig played Vic and Bob and were flat out hilarious – at one point they did a joke about Mr Martin's pubes and got away with it. Another kid nailed it as George Doors, they had the Dove from Above; a nerdy kid called Matthew played the Geek of the Week and danced sideways across the stage while the rest of his class sang 'Geek of the Week' and he totally owned it to the point where everyone in our year respected him and I'm pretty sure no one ever gave him any grief for being a geek ever again. For the rest of the day all I did was think about how funny that assembly had been and how much I wished my class had done something like that. The good news was that next Monday it was my class's turn to do the assembly and we were all in agreement: we had to do something as funny as *Shooting Stars*.

We did struggle to think of something radically different to be honest. We knew it was really funny that they had recreated a TV show in their assembly and we all wanted to do the same, but we couldn't agree on a specific show to send up so we compromised and decided that our assembly would consist of one of us playing somebody watching TV and flicking through the channels and the rest of us would act out all the different shows. Ambitious but potentially a good idea. So we divided into groups of four with each group assigned a TV show which they were to write a sketch about.

My group were given *EastEnders*. I personally have never seen *EastEnders*. Still to this day I've never seen it. Back then I'd never seen it AND I was eleven, so wasn't as good at guessing what *EastEnders* might be like as I am now. All I knew was that Mr Martin's class were funny so we better be funny. I asked the other kids in my group what was going on in *EastEnders* right now.

'Ian Beale is obsessed with the environment and being green,' said Joseph. 'The Mitchell brothers are beating people up,' said Luke.

I nodded and began to write. I had to make this good, I couldn't have another Cub Scout Circus Show or *Woodcutter and the Christmas Dove* on my hands. This had to be so funny that everyone would forget all about *Shooting Stars*. I did what I should've done when I learned to juggle and I followed my instincts. As I read it back to myself I knew this would be even funnier than actual *EastEnders* itself. And I had written it in five minutes flat. Three minutes longer than it took me to learn to juggle. Because if you want a job done well you've got to put the time in.

Monday rolled around and it was time for the big assembly. The rest of our year were sat on the floor, cross legged, waiting to watch what we'd come up with; some of the kids were still reminiscing about how incredible *Shooting Stars* had been the week before. The kids who put on the *Shooting Stars* assembly were sitting in the audience too, looking like bona fide celebs, lapping up the praise. Well, enjoy it while it lasts, because now it's our turn to shine.

One of my classmates walked out onstage, sat on a chair and pretended to flick through TV channels with a remote control. Each time they pressed a button, a different kid would rush out and say a couple of words, imitating something from a TV show (this was just to establish the premise, no big laughs just yet) and then we moved on to some longer sketches. To be honest, I can't remember what any of the other kids' sketches were, what shows they were sending up, who was in them – nothing. All I was focused on was how much we were about to melt people's minds with the *EastEnders* sketch that I had written all by myself, without any help from anyone else. Just me.

All I know is the sketch before us ended and that was our cue to begin.

Luke and Leavan walked on to the stage as the Mitchell Brothers, talking to each other like tough guys. The audience were silent, taking in all the info while we set the scene for them. Then, from the other side of the stage, I entered, playing the role of Ian Beale, wearing a big green padded coat. As we crossed paths the Mitchells threw a chocolate bar wrapper on the floor. I stopped in my tracks, staring at the litter in disgust.

'Oi!' I shouted. 'Are you going to pick that up?'

'No,' said Phil Mitchell.

'Pick it up!' I retorted.

'What you gonna do about it?' said Grant Mitchell.

'Nothing!' I boomed. 'But...' and then I ran offstage.

The room was silent for about thirty seconds and then... I returned! Running full pelt back on to the stage, having taken my big green coat off and tied it around my neck like a cape, '... Eco Man will!' I shouted to utter silence.

Then, with my hands on my hips, I continued, 'You messed with Eco Man and his sidekick – The Bin Bag!' Then my friend Joe ran onstage wearing a bin bag (we had cut a hole in the bottom of the bin bag and put it over his head like a poncho).

The Bin Bag made a high-pitched noise that sounded like, 'Meep Moop!' Also to silence.

What followed was a ten-minute-long comedy fight where Eco Man and The Bin Bag beat up the Mitchell Brothers and every time I punched someone I would shout 'Eco Man!' really fast while The Bin Bag ran around, constantly making Pingu-type noises. This entire fight sequence also played to silence. The sketch ended with the Mitchell Brothers in a pile on the floor, me with my foot up on their lifeless bodies, The Bin Bag doing a victory dance next to me, to pure and perfect silence.

The Bin Bag

Every single person in the school year had watched the entire sketch without making a peep. They hadn't laughed or, to be fair, heckled; they just stared at us, trying to figure out what they'd just seen. Because (and I only realised this once we were onstage performing the sketch for the first time), we hadn't established that the programme we were sending up was

EastEnders. At no point did we tell the audience that this was meant to be *EastEnders*. We didn't use the *EastEnders* theme music at the start of the sketch and we didn't say any of the characters' names at any point, so no one knew we were Ian Beale and the Mitchell Brothers; as far as our audience were concerned they had just seen us perform a note perfect version of an obscure show called 'Eco Man' that actually existed.

After the performance one of the girls who'd been in the audience asked me where they could watch the original TV show. I told them we were doing *EastEnders* and I was playing Ian Beale and finally I achieved the laughter I had been so very hungry for while on stage. She told some other girls and they found it equally hysterical. I was pretty sure they weren't laughing for the right reasons and the reasons they were laughing for were probably bad, but at this point I'd take anything. For about six months after that those girls would call me Ian Beale (or his alter ego, Eco Man) in the corridor whenever they walked past. And yeah it was pretty mean of them but I'll say this – Mr Martin's class never got 'Shooting Stars' yelled at them on the way to their maths lesson. So maybe I could console myself with that? At least my work was standing the test of time. Come to think of it, it's not like Matthew had been able to follow up his Cub Scout Circus Show juggling act – he'd been a flash in the pan! Little did I know that I was about to experience a hit of my own and I'd soon discover that being a big success wasn't all it was cracked up to be.

Humpty Dumpty

Only a few weeks later during a music lesson, my class were split into groups of five or six, sent to different rooms and told to choose any genre of music, then take a nursery rhyme and perform it in our chosen genre. My friends and I proceeded to joke around and not do any work and then when we were told we only had two minutes left we quickly threw something together. I was unaware at the time that what we had thrown together was both the best and worst thing I had ever had a hand in (this is probably still the case even now).

The nursery rhyme we chose was 'Humpty Dumpty', the instruments we chose were our voices. We were the only group in the class to go completely a cappella. We watched as the other groups performed their nursery rhymes for the class and the standard was high. A reggae version of 'Little Bo Peep' was very well received and a hip-hop 'Grand Old Duke of York' set people's hearts on fire. We were the final group to perform (some would call us the headliners but I don't like to say that as it sounds like boasting but yes we were technically the headliners). My four friends (three of whom were the same friends from the ill-fated Eco Man sketch) stood behind me in a line, shoulder to shoulder, and began to sway from side to side while reciting 'Humpty Dumpty' slowly and sadly in a depressing monotone.

Meanwhile, I paced back and forth in front of them, rubbing my brow as though terribly vexed, speaking the nursery rhyme out loud, one line at a time, leaving weird pauses throughout, much like William Shatner (although I didn't know who William Shatner was at the time so you could say I invented this way of speaking). My friends got quieter and quieter until it was just me speaking dramatically (my first solo since *Woodcutter*) until I said, with some weight, '... couldn't... put Humpty... together... again.'

I then looked at our audience solemnly, letting those words sink in, and then, with gusto, and to the tune of the worldwide hit 'La Bamba', I sang, 'La-la-la-la-la-la Humpty!' My backing singers immediately responded with 'Humpty Dumpty' then me, 'Sat on a wall!' then them, 'Sat on a wall!'

'La-la-la-la-la-la Humpty now!'

'Humpty Dumpty.'

'I said he had a great fall!'

My backing singers were now dancing behind me; I believe it was a dance known as The Mashed Potato, and I was doing some enthusiastic air guitar (bearing in mind that some of our fellow classmates had actually bothered to play a real guitar for their songs so me choosing to air-guitar was pretty rich), headbanging and putting my foot up on any desks and chairs nearby as if they were monitors. And, against all the odds, the crowd went berserk. I had never experienced a reaction like it.

Our fellow classmates were laughing, clapping, having the time of their lives. The chorus consisted of my backing singers singing, 'La la Humpty' over and over again with me shouting things like 'Humpty!' and 'Humpty Dumpty!' in the gaps; on more than one occasion I remember shouting, 'That egg man!' at the top of my lungs. We had not discussed how we would end the song. The performance went on for over ten minutes and, as far as I can remember, only got better with every passing second. I particularly enjoyed singing about all the king's horses and all the king's men and how they couldn't put Humpty together again, throwing in various 'nows' and 'oh yeahs' for good measure – 'You know that all the king's horses now... oh yeah and all the king's men!' – and repeating 'That egg man!' several times whenever the mood took me.

Looking back, I am surprised our teacher did not put a stop to this sooner. Maybe, like us, she had also under-prepared for the lesson and was just happy to let us eat up some time with the longest, most repetitive song ever written. Eventually she had to step in, placing her hand on my shoulder and saying, 'I think that's all of the nursery rhyme isn't it?' and my headbanging slowed down and I raised my arms as I accepted my classmate's deafening applause.

The next music lesson we had wasn't as fun as the nursery rhyme lesson as we didn't get to play any music, just write about music and copy stuff from the board. Our teacher could tell that our attention was waning so announced that once we'd all done our work we could all choose an instrument to play as a reward.

But the class didn't want to play any instruments and they made that known rather swiftly. 'Can we have a different reward, miss?'

'Like what?'

There was a pause and then, 'Can we watch "La La La Humpty" again?'

This, I should point out, was a request from someone *not* in the band – this was a fan. And everybody else in the class agreed that watching us perform 'La La La Humpty' for a second time was much better than getting to play musical instruments themselves.

'James, is that OK?' the teacher asked, and I remember saying yes like I was a world renowned superstar who doesn't mind doing something nice for his public, all cool, shrugging my shoulders. 'Yeah, sure.'

Everyone cheered and I felt like a real big deal. You have never seen a class of eleven-year-olds work as hard as my class did in music that day. Heads down, pens constantly moving, pages turning, learning like heck. We had a collective goal and nothing was going to get in our way. We finished the work with twenty minutes to spare, which meant we could've crammed two performances of 'La La La Humpty' in if we'd felt so inclined. As soon as the final student closed their workbook, true to her word, our teacher introduced us on to the stage (the bit of carpet in front of the class). I can't remember if the band had a name or not. Some good names would've been:

We Are The Egg Men
All The King's Legends
Rumpty Pumpty
Nursery Crimes
Sunny Side Up

The Great Fall (a play on pre-existing band name, The Fall)
Five Eggs One Basket
The Yolk Singers
Easter 17

But we were probably just known as James and his Friends.

The second performance of 'La La La Humpty' was almost more electric than the first (as if such a thing were possible). Back when we had performed the sad, slow intro to the song for the *first* time, none of our audience knew what was coming. But this time they all knew where we were heading, so throughout the entire intro-duction everybody in the room was grinning and shifting about with excitement, anticipating the moment they were all waiting for, and the closer we got to me shouting 'La-la-la-la-la-la Humpty', the more the room fizzed and buzzed with unbridled giddiness. In fact when I did shout 'La-la-la-la-la-la Humpty' there wasn't a single person who didn't totally lose control (teacher included), and in the end we didn't need to perform the song twice because when you've got that much love coming back to the stage from the crowd, it's very easy to make 'La La La Humpty' last just under twenty minutes.

I'm not going to undersell this; when we finished performing 'La La La Humpty' for the second time I felt invincible. They loved us, they really loved us. We had experienced crushing failure in the world of sketch comedy but had found our true calling in the world of music parody. My days of playing Ian Beale were behind me; I was a singer now. And let's not forget that singing in front of people was no small thing for me. I had completely frozen up when singing 'A Woodcutter's Prayer' in primary school, paralysed with fear. But now I wasn't just singing, I was singing a cappella, I was singing lead vocals in an a cappella group and

I was doing so with confidence and finesse. But the elation was short lived.

During a maths lesson, our class was once again promised a reward if we finished our work (I believe we would've been allowed to go on the computers). I wasn't expecting this request outside of music class but, once again, a fellow classmate raised their hand and asked if instead of computer time, they could all enjoy a third rendition of 'La La La Humpty' by James and his Friends. The maths teacher did not know what this was so she had to have it explained to her. I can't remember who described 'La La La Humpty' to our maths teacher but I wish I had recorded it: an eleven year old explaining an a cappella rock version of a children's nursery rhyme to an adult, all the time trying to sell the idea as best they can in order to be able to watch the song live as a reward.

'Miss, imagine if you will the nursery rhyme "Humpty Dumpty". Now imagine the song "La La La Bamba". Now combine the two. So, you can probably understand why this matters so much to us.' After the explanation she somehow still agreed to let 'La La La Humpty' be our *maths class* reward.

Now, it's not that the audience didn't love it the third time because, believe you me, they absolutely did, but I could feel my enthusiasm beginning to sap when I performed 'La La La Humpty' at the end of maths class that day. My bandmates still seemed to be revelling in the limelight, but for some reason my energy was slipping. Maybe it was the fact we were performing in a maths classroom, the acoustics more suited to silence than banging tunes, but I just wasn't feeling it. Please understand that, like a true pro, I didn't let it show; as far as the audience were concerned I was still unreservedly rocking out to the memory of Humpty Dumpty aka That Egg Man (the third time round and some of the class joined in with 'That egg man' whenever I shouted it). I may have been dead on the inside but I couldn't let our loyal fanbase down, especially after they'd worked so hard in maths class and finished all their sums.

I suppose this is something all celebrities go through at some stage, especially musicians; you have your original big hit and you welcome the fame at first, but before long you feel like a performing monkey, like you're a slave to your audience, and that no one really seems to care about the real you, all they see is a superstar and not a human being.

'La La La Humpty' became the class reward for every single lesson we had together. I would dread hearing the teacher say there would be a reward at the end of class. I would try and distract other pupils from their work so we didn't all finish on time, but to no avail. It turns out that children are most focused once they've been promised another reprise of 'La La La Humpty'. The performance would always take it out of me, emotionally and physically. I had to start the song in a really sad place and then launch into a full body workout for nine minutes minimum every time. And even though 'La La La Humpty' had been a roaring success, we seemed unable to follow it up with another hit. Trying to reproduce that winning formula felt impossible. Upon reflection, we probably only ever performed it five times, but it felt like a world tour.

It was during another performance in the music class that I finally broke. The teacher had stopped asking what we wanted as our reward by this point as it was a given that we would choose 'La La La Humpty'. We stood in front of the class and, to begin with, all was well. We did the sad bit flawlessly, but maybe a little too flawlessly. I felt the sadness for real this time. It cut to the core of me and as my backing singers faded away and I was left to launch into the song I got as far as 'La-la-la-

la-la-la Hum—' before my voice cracked, I felt all my confidence evaporate, and suddenly I felt like I was dressed as a woodcutter again, holding a plastic axe and a toy dove, scared to make a sound. I let out a sigh and, exhausted, turned to my teacher and regretfully said, 'I'm sorry, miss, but I can't do this any more.'

The class let out a disappointed and slightly angry 'aaaawww' before the teacher held her hands up and said, 'No, don't make him do it if he doesn't want to.'

I turned and looked at my bandmates. They were confused but also appeared slightly relieved. They had never vocalised any complaints but it must've been tough to stand up there day after day, singing their hearts out while I took all the glory. Those guys still mean the world to me and I wish them all the happiness and success this crazy world has to offer.

We never had to perform 'La La La Humpty' again. Rewards went back to normal things like drawing or, if you were the class bully, basically being let off the leash to do whatever you felt like doing. We were one hit wonders, but we had to remember that most people don't even get to achieve one hit, and what we had was special and that time was precious. I know that now. One day, if I have children of my own, maybe I'll read them the story of 'Humpty Dumpty' and if they ask then I'll say, 'Yes. I did write an a cappella version of this nursery rhyme that captured the hearts and minds of a generation.' And remember, the pupils in my year seven class worked hard to hear that song every day. Because of me, a whole classroom of children learned more than they would've had I not been there. And although I may not have gone to university, some of my classmates did, and I like to think that when they graduated they laughed to themselves, shook their heads and, smiling, whispered, 'That egg man.'

School Band

'La La La Humpty' had given me a taste for performing live music (plus I already played the drums) and so I joined the school band. There were loads of kids in the band playing all sorts of brass, wind, string and percussive instruments but they didn't have a drummer, so my music teacher suggested I gave it a go. I loved it, and when I was fourteen we went on the best school trip ever – a school band trip to Holland. The school band, school choir and a contemporary covers band would travel around Holland and get to perform three gigs along the way. I was playing drums in both the school band and the covers band. We went to a theme park at one point and went on an amazing ride. It was part roller coaster, part bobsled run – one minute you were on tracks then the next you were free-falling through a tunnel. It was one of the most exhilarating roller coasters I've ever been on (no offence to Wicksteed Park and the Pinfari roller coaster, still forever in my heart and always on my mind).

We also got to stay at loads of great hostels and hotels. One place we stayed at had a caged parrot in the foyer. After a couple of nights we all noticed that every night at six p.m. the parrot would get taken away and would reappear in the foyer at nine a.m. the next morning. We asked the owner where the parrot went after six o'clock and he smiled, mimed snapping the parrot's neck, made a neck-snapping sound effect and said, 'Parrot soup!' We all laughed.

'No, seriously though, where does the parrot go?' one of the sixth formers asked. The owner mimed snapping the parrot's neck, made a neck-snapping sound effect and said, 'Parrot soup!' We all laughed again. Nice one.

'OK but seriously, where does the parrot go?' asked the same sixth former. The owner smiled, mimed snapping the parrot's neck, made a neck-snapping sound effect and said, 'Parrot soup!' About two kids laughed.

'Where does the parrot go at six p.m.?' asked the same sixth former. The owner mimed snapping the parrot's neck, made a neck-snapping sound effect and said, 'Parrot soup!' Nobody laughed. The owner, however, looked delighted with himself. He was clearly joking and still found it hilarious regardless of the audience's response.

'Yeah but it always comes back in the morning so we know you don't make parrot soup out of it, so where does it go?'

The owner nodded then mimed snapping the parrot's neck, made a neck-snapping sound effect and said, 'Parrot soup!' Two kids laughed, unable to believe he was still doing the parrot soup joke after it had got nothing the last time, but as far as the owner was concerned two laughs meant he was winning us back. The sixth former lost it.

'You don't make parrot soup out of it mate, we just want to know where the parrot goes at night, that's all!' The owner looked surprised by the sixth former's latest outburst, paused and then mimed snapping the parrot's neck, made a neck-snapping sound effect and said, 'Parrot soup!' Everybody, except for the sixth former, laughed again. It was pure genius of him to do it again, we loved it – to keep on pushing!

'Right. Just please tell us where the parrot goes at six o'clock every night and do not say parrot soup again!'

The owner nodded, a serious expression on his face. He understood this wasn't funny any more. He held up his hands to show he knew he'd been out of order. And then he paused, leaned in and mimed snapping the parrot's neck, made a neck-snapping sound effect and said, 'Parrot soup!' We didn't stop laughing at this one for a full five minutes, the owner just standing there looking chuffed with himself.

This went on for nearly an hour. Sometimes the conversation would drift away from the parrot and we'd talk about other stuff. He'd share with us stories of his life, his relationships, growing up, and when he appeared to have dropped his guard someone would say, 'So, come on, seriously, where do you put the parrot at six o'clock?' And he'd lean in, mime snapping the parrot's neck, make a neck-snapping sound effect and say, 'Parrot soup!' And we'd either laugh or get insanely irritated with him. Either way he was always fully satisfied with our reaction.

Naturally many kids took to asking the parrot itself in the daytime; they'd ask it where it went at six o'clock but it never replied. Although, I would bet money that whenever we were out of the hotel the owner was trying to teach it to say 'Parrot soup'.

The only time I have ever laughed more than at Parrot Soup was during a family day out in Banbury. It was lunchtime and we went to a quaint little tea shop. The tea room was empty, and we sat on a round table in the corner and ordered Banbury cakes and cups of tea for the table. The little old lady who owned the tea shop returned ten minutes later with our tea and cakes. She handed them out to us all one by one. The last person to receive his cake was my brother, who was sat across the table from where she was standing. She looked at him, said, 'Here's your Banbury cake,' then as she leant across the table to hand him the plate, she did a really loud fart. I have never laughed as hard as I did when that old lady farted. The fart wasn't the funniest part, it was what she said before the fart: 'Here's your Banbury cake.' She looked at him, said, 'Here's your Banbury cake' and then farted. Even though it was accidental, the phrase made it seem like she meant to do it. When giving food to a stranger! And she looked at him before she did it, like a cold-hearted killer. Tears were streaming down my mother's face she was laughing so much. When you're a kid, seeing your mum or dad laughing at something you're also laughing at just makes you laugh even more, maybe because sharing that connection with your parents naturally makes you happier. I hurt so much from laughing. I can't even remember if the lady had left the table or not. Here's your Banbury cake. Lord have mercy.

I loved playing in both bands on the Holland tour. I remember everyone had to dress smart for the performances. A lot of the boys wore ties but I didn't because I'd never tied a tie before and for some reason didn't feel like learning now. Thanks to this attitude I would never even attempt to tie a tie until I was twenty-eight years old.

I never went to a school that had a tie in the uniform (just the kind where you have to bring a towel in with you every day. 'All towels and no ties' – that was my school motto) and when I had to wear a tie for weddings, funerals or christenings someone would just do it for me because we were in too much of a rush for them to teach me. But when I was twenty-eight I got invited to a wedding back home in Kettering and was now at a stage where I didn't even *own* a tie; that's how much I'd given up on learning how to tie one. I was meant to be borrowing a tie from my flatmate but when I was leaving in the morning he was still asleep and I didn't want to wake him so decided to buy one when I arrived in Kettering as I would be arriving with plenty of time to spare. The plan went swimmingly to begin with.

I arrived in Kettering, headed straight to M&S, bought a tie and left. It was only when I got outside that I remembered I'd never tied a tie in my entire life. So, naturally, I went on my phone and Googled 'How to tie a tie' and selected the clearest step-by-step diagram to walk me through it. This was all well and good but I wanted to tie the tie in private and not out in the street where everyone could see me struggle. After much consideration, my options appeared to be a) the toilets in the shopping centre or b) the fitting rooms in any number of clothing stores nearby. I decided the toilets were too gross so I went to TK Maxx to use their fitting rooms. Obviously it is impossible to gain access to the fitting rooms without an item of clothing from the store you are currently in so I grabbed a shirt off the rack and walked right into my own private fitting room. I hung the shirt up immediately, got the tie ready, got my phone out and studied the diagram.

Now, when you've never tied a tie before, tying a tie is really hard. It felt exactly like being a little kid learning how to tie my shoelaces and feeling like I was never going to get my head round this abstract concept; how was I ever meant to fathom such a complex technique? With every failed attempt I got more and more stressed out because I knew the lady who allowed me into the fitting rooms would be wondering what the hold-up was. I began to wish I'd brought in more items of clothing to justify being in here for so long. Tying a tie for the first time when you're twenty-eight is like never watching a single film until you're twenty-eight and then trying to watch and understand *2001: A Space Odyssey*. You're having to pause and rewind constantly, you have no frame of reference for anything that's happening in front of you, none of it makes sense on any level. The dishonest fitting room situation made this even worse. Imagine you've gone into a cinema that was meant to be showing *The Tigger Movie* but you're secretly watching *2001: A Space Odyssey* in there while the staff wait for you outside and are wondering why you've been in there for three hours when *The Tigger Movie* only lasts one hour and twenty minutes.

After multiple failed attempts to tie the tie, each attempt more frantic and infuriating than the last, I composed myself and tried again, taking my time, focusing on each step, trusting the diagram and, somehow, I got it right. I emerged from the fitting room carrying the shirt and, curiously, wearing a tie that I wasn't wearing before entering the fitting room. The lady seemed to notice this but also seemed to acknowledge that the tie was not from TK Maxx and so didn't bring it up. I don't know if this had ever happened to her before. Do people regularly go into the TK Maxx fitting rooms and emerge wearing brand new clothing from another store instead of the outfit they went in to try? Maybe TK Maxx employees have accepted by now that their fitting rooms are more popular than their actual clothes and have decided to allow customers from other stores to make use of their first class facilities regardless of the fact they haven't sold a shirt in months. Maybe it had never happened before but she just decided she couldn't do with the inevitable hassle of getting to the bottom of this particular mystery. She would've had to interrogate me for ages and at the end would just have learnt the one thing she knew all along – that I was a very odd man.

'Were you happy with the shirt, sir?'

'No, it's not for me I don't think,' I said, pretty convincingly I might add.

'Oh? What exactly were you looking for?' She beckoned a colleague over who joined her and they both looked at me intently, keen to hear what sort of a shirt I was looking to buy that day, which of course I wasn't because I only wanted to use the fitting rooms so I could teach myself how to tie a tie in private away from the prying eyes of the general public.

'Blue... plain blue... nothing too tight...' I kept adding adjectives hoping they'd leave me alone but each one just got me in more and more trouble until I eventually ended up *buying* a plain blue baggy shirt with a medium sized collar and small buttons for a reasonable price, not too shiny.

It's worth pointing out that in order to buy a shirt I had to try on a shirt, which meant I had to take off the shirt *and tie* I currently had on. I very nearly completely untied the tie in order to do this before remembering how to loosen it. If I had untied it and had to re-tie it again afterwards then this story may well have gone on forever. I wouldn't have been able to re-tie the tie in TK Maxx because that would've taken ages and I needed to get out of there ASAP, so I would've ended up buying the TK Maxx shirt then running over to H&M to use their fitting room to re-tie the tie, and I'd have to take a shirt in with me, and I'd once again take ages to tie the tie, then inevitably get roped into buying another shirt, which means I'd have to try it on, which means I'd have to untie the tie again, so I'd have to leave H&M and quickly nip into Next to use their fitting rooms instead, and on and on and so on and so forth. By the end of it I would've arrived at that wedding wearing twenty shirts and no tie. Sometimes it's good to remind myself that things could've gone a lot worse; it makes me feel much better about buying a shirt I didn't need.

Pindrop

After the tour of Holland I spent all my time at secondary school trying to get people to form bands with me but to no avail (it's hard to be taken seriously when you were the 'La La La Humpty' kid. And also Eco Man.) When I was fifteen I finally formed my first band, a nu metal outfit by the name of Pindrop. Nu metal is a genre that usually mixes metal with hip hop resulting in something that doesn't sound as good as metal or hip hop. A lot of nu metal bands had the kind of name where you put two one-syllable words together to form a new word and 'Pindrop' was an absolute classic. You can do it with anything though: Gnomelord, Yakblood, Yaklord, Gnomeblood, Gnomeyak, Gnomedrop, Pinyak – the possibilities are endless.

There were four of us in the band – drums, two guitarists and a bass player – but none of us sang. There was no way in hell I was going to put myself forward to do vocal duty, no way no how. I don't think I need to explain why to you either – if I wasn't totally freezing up during the school play, I was belting out a nursery rhyme and becoming a slave to my own success. Nope, I'd learnt my lesson. But we were always looking for a singer and in our one year of playing gigs we went through several, the most noteworthy of which was Lloyd.

Lloyd was the perfect nu metal singer. He looked real cool (lip piercing, hair gelled into big spikes, symmetrical face) and could actually sing. There were a few different types of nu metal singer: rapper ones, nice sing-y ones, screamy ones, and any combination of the three. We wanted a nice sing-y one and Lloyd was just that. We had some top-notch band practices and he sounded spot on.

Our first gig with Lloyd was in a youth centre, in the back room where boxing classes usually took place, which meant the stage was a boxing ring. You're right, that is the coolest thing you've ever heard. (What's even cooler is the fact that this ended up being the final gig held in the boxing ring because shortly afterwards the youth centre received a health and safety inspection and were told by the fire safety guy that the room we'd been having gigs in was officially 'a bloody death trap'.) We were the second band on that night, and although Lloyd seemed nervous we had full faith in him.

As I was setting up my drum kit he said to me, 'You guys start playing the first song without me and I'll come on later. Just keep playing that opening riff until I get onstage, OK?' We hadn't practised opening our set like this but it sounded like a nifty idea so we all agreed to give it a go. Obviously I was familiar with the technique Lloyd was suggesting: start off with a repetitive, almost boring refrain and then bring in the lead vocalist and completely change everything, resulting in pandemonium – sound familiar?[2]

And so at the start of our gig, the four of us began playing the opening riff to the first song. Then we repeated that riff, really building up the tension in the room, getting the crowd on tenterhooks. Then we repeated it again. At this point we were visibly looking around, trying to locate Lloyd, but he was nowhere to be seen. If he'd run away we had no backup plan. The riff was starting to wear thin now. The crowd were being nice, nodding their heads in time with the beat, but it was clear that they were patiently waiting for us to play something that wasn't this riff.

But just when I started to believe he had definitely deserted us, Lloyd entered the ring. He had gone and got changed into a floral dress, something we weren't aware he was going to do but that seemed kind of nifty; we were a nu metal band and we had a cool looking singer wearing a dress usually worn by elderly women – fuck the system. He picked up the mic, the crowd moving about a bit more now – this guy had stage presence, no question about it. He lifted the mic to his lips and we prepared ourselves for those sweet melodic vocals.

And then he shouted into the mic for half an hour.

From start to finish, just shouting. Not even in the same rhythm as the vocals he'd done in band practice, and not good shouting either, just unpleasant shouting like an old man with no teeth yelling at you for parking your car in front of his house.

---

2 I am referring to 'La La La Humpty'.

After the gig ended, we were standing outside while our lead guitarist was smoking.

'That was fun,' said Lloyd. We shuffled around, looking at our feet.

'Yeah...' we all mumbled, unconvincingly.

'Those vocals were different, Lloyd,' I said.

'Did you like them?' he asked, and our guitarist, a boy by the name of Butler, fifteen years old but with a better beard than I can now grow at thirty-two, answered, 'Not really. Do the proper singing next like you did in practice, mate,' and the rest of us nodded while still avoiding eye contact. A look of understanding swept over Lloyd's face and he responded in a surprisingly mature manner.

'Of course, yeah you're right, sorry guys, I don't know why I surprised you like that, I'll do proper singing next time, won't happen again.' Cool.

Our second gig was in a traditional English pub. Lloyd showed up, this time not wearing his dress, but once again appeared nervous. We'd had some good practices in between gigs, with Lloyd singing very sweetly, and we were looking forward to gig number two. Before we went on, Lloyd came up to me.

'Hey, you guys start the first song without me and I'll come on later, OK?'

I paused and looked at him uncertainly. He instantly read my mind.

'I won't shout again I promise, man,' he said. 'Look I'm really sorry about what happened last time, I shouldn't have tried something new without asking you guys and you're totally right it sounds better when I sing nicely. Honestly, it won't happen again, I don't know what got into me, to be honest.'

I nodded, the kind of nod you do when you're trying to convince yourself that everything is fine by forcing your brain to move your head in a way that you've come to associate with everything being fine. 'OK, all good.'

Lloyd smiled. 'Great.'

Pindrop took to the stage, we played the intro for a while, then a while longer, and then Lloyd ran onstage wearing his floral dress. OK, I thought to myself, *the dress is fine, we didn't say don't wear the dress anymore, we actually like the dress, it's just that at the last gig the dress was the first of two surprises and the second one was very much unwanted. But just because he's wearing the dress does not mean he's about to shout – the dress could just be his stage outfit; we don't know because we've never discussed it as a band because we're all fifteen and haven't learned tactful ways of bringing these kind of things up yet but just because he's wearing the dress doesn't mean he's about to do shouting again.*

And then he did shouting again. For the entire set, jumping around the stage, leaping as high as he could in the air and every time he landed he'd stick his middle finger up at the audience. Every time. Just shouting and flipping people off for a full thirty minutes then throwing the mic on the ground and running off stage again.

Once again we found ourselves standing outside after the gig, this time all looking at Lloyd with anger in our eyes.

'I know,' said Lloyd, holding his hands up, 'I'm sorry, I know that wasn't the plan, it just felt right at the time but I see now it wasn't the right thing to do.'

Butler looked like he was about to punch him. 'Just... don't do it again, Lloyd.'

'I won't. You have my word. I will never ever do it again.'

*

Our third gig was in a community centre on the outskirts of town. We'd had some nice practices with Lloyd in between the second and third gig, with him singing very sweetly indeed but with us eyeing him with suspicion every time. Every practice would end with us saying to him, 'And that's how you're going to sing at the next gig, isn't it?' and he'd reassure us.

'Absolutely, I promise, I can't apologise enough for last time.'

Now it was gig night and we were all on edge, more so than ever before. Lloyd, on the other hand, was cool as a cucumber. As we were setting up, Lloyd came up to me.

'Hey, you guys start the first song without me and I'll come on later, yeah?'

I looked at him for a long time, without speaking. 'And then what are you going to do?'

He looked back at me like he literally had no idea what I was talking about. 'I'll just come on and sing, properly.'

Another pause. 'Will you?'

Lloyd looked at me with a face like butter wouldn't melt. 'Yeah man, just like we practised.'

I went back to setting up my drums but turned back to face Lloyd after less than a second. 'Because at the last two gigs you've told us to start without you and then you've run on and done shouting.'

He nodded disapprovingly as if we were both on the same team and were bollocking somebody else. 'Those days are behind me now, I'm going to sing tonight, I am.'

I looked at him with urgency in my eyes. 'You're definitely going to sing?'

'Definitely.'

We looked at each other for quite some time. 'OK, fine.'

And so we started playing the intro to the first song. And we carried on playing the intro to the first song. Lloyd was nowhere to be seen. This was the longest we'd ever played the intro for. Where was he? After a full five minutes of playing the same riff over and over, we saw him. Bounding towards the stage in another floral dress. With a dick drawn across his forehead in eyeliner pencil. Just a full dick and balls drawn across his forehead. I had so much hope in my heart that he had decided to trade the shouting for the dick. Like maybe singing nicely with a dick drawn on your forehead is akin to simply shouting for the whole set? But another part of me, quite a big part of me, saw the dick as a bad sign. People who draw dicks on their foreheads are rarely on their best behaviour. As he got closer my faith waned more and more. He reached the stage, picked up the mic and sang incredibly beautifully for the first time ever.

Only joking. He screamed for thirty minutes. Screaming is way worse than shouting, by the way. At one point he took the dress off completely (he was wearing boxers), revealing that he'd also written 'SUZEE WOZ ERE' across his stomach with an arrow pointing down to his penis (his actual penis, not the one drawn across his forehead.) Who was Suzee? Suzee was a friend of his; she was in the audience and was the only person enjoying the set. I'm fairly certain she's the one who drew all that stuff on him in the first place. He didn't even try and sing and then resort to screaming; he just launched straight into it like it was plan A (which it clearly was) and we just had to keep on playing the songs. At the end of every song he would raise his arms in the air like a boxer who's just won a fight, but to zero applause. He was 'Ian Beale-ing' pretty badly, as we say in the industry. He had to go.

We fired him eventually but it took weeks because there was never a good time. We wanted to do it straight after the gig but couldn't because Lloyd got headbutted (by some troublemakers for no reason. Nothing to do with his performance) and it felt cruel to fire him while his nose was bleeding. The person who headbutted him ran away immediately, which I was disappointed about. Ever since, I've desperately wanted to know if the head-butter ended up with a faded dick printed backwards across his forehead.

Jam

Around the same time I was in Pindrop, I would regularly attend a jam night in Kettering. It took place every Tuesday and for a young musician like me it was everything I needed: a place to meet other musicians, some of them new, some of them more experienced (old, I'm trying to say old), and learn how to play with other people, how to listen to other players and develop my skills as a drummer. Most of the people who went there were in their forties and fifties, with only a handful of youngsters like me attending each week. I'd often be able to get up and play one or two songs, try and show off as much as I could, and then sit down. The jam night switched venues quite a lot in those days but on this particular night it was being held at The Poppies Social Club, a small bar just off the side of the Kettering football ground. I turned up to find that there were no youngsters present that day. This meant it would take me longer to get on because usually I'd just get up with a bunch of people my age as we were all at a similar level in terms of ability. I sat and watched as musicians rotated, playing a lot of blues and rock, until I got called on to fill in on the drums for a song. Sitting down behind the drums at the jam night was always a slightly nerve-wracking experience. I had no idea what they were about to play and I was keen to impress the older guys by playing a beat they perhaps didn't expect. I really felt like I had to prove myself. The guitarist started playing the opening riff to what I now know was 'All Along The Watchtower', the Jimi Hendrix version.

However, when I was sixteen I had never listened to 'All Along The Watchtower', so as far as I was concerned, this man was just jamming out with a riff he had made up on the spot. I have to say, I was impressed. I really dug it. This guy had some skills – what a beautiful song to make up so effortlessly. It truly was an honour to jam out alongside him. But now I had to join in on the drums. I listened to the riff and thought it sounded pretty bluesy, pretty rocky, but all the drummers before me had played a blues or rock beat and I had to show these guys what I was made of in order to stand out from the crowd. So I played a disco beat. Sixteenths on the hi-hat, funky and dance-y all the way, and as far as I was concerned it worked, it worked very nicely indeed. You might not believe that it worked very nicely indeed but imagine that you've never heard 'All Along The Watchtower' before, and the first time you hear it, it's got a disco beat. You wouldn't think it was awful, you'd actually think it was a pretty great song.

However, I am the only person this has ever happened to and

probably the only person it will ever happen to because no other musician would dream of mixing Hendrix with disco and I was the only person in The Poppies Social Club that evening who had never heard 'All Along the Watchtower'. I was grooving away, opening and shutting the hi-hat on the off-beats, but when I looked up and around the room for the first time the reception appeared hostile.

The musicians I was playing with looked less than pleased. They were all standing awkwardly, with rigid posture as if they were being forced to play the song against their will, and the audience were all staring daggers at me, older men in flat caps gripping their pints until their knuckles turned white, glaring at this young buck on the drums. But I couldn't change now, I had to keep going. The vocalist began to sing what to my ears was a very pleasing melody, so surely that would calm people down. I started listening to the vocals and then heard him sing a familiar line (the lyric in question being 'All along the watchtower') and I thought, *Oh no. I've heard of that.*

Now I hadn't ever sat down and properly listened to 'All Along the Watchtower', and I certainly didn't recognise the riff straight away, but when I heard the title of the song sung by the lead vocalist then you better believe I realised there and then that I was currently turning the timeless classic 'All Along the Watchtower' into a Bee Gees tune in front of people to whom the song meant a great deal. I wracked my brains to try and remember who the song was by and when I remembered, my panic levels shot through the roof. The only thing worse than realising you're currently ruining a song by Jimi Hendrix is realising you're currently ruining a song by Jimi Hendrix *and* Bob Dylan. Two of the all-time greats butchered with one damn funky beat (and it was damn funky). They cut the song short (not that I had any idea, my dad was watching from the back and told me afterwards), and another drummer was ushered hastily towards the kit. As I was putting my sticks back in my bag two people came up to me, one by one. The first was an angry looking old boy, pint in hand, who told me in a slow and raspy voice, 'No one – NO ONE – plays a disco beat to "All Along the Watchtower".' And I nodded because I had already figured that out all by myself.

The second man to approach me described my take on the song as, 'One of the most horrifying things I've ever witnessed.' That sounds pretty extreme as it is, but even more so when you consider that the jam night took place on (and remember that everything in this book is true) 11 September 2001. On the actual day itself. There was footage of New York being shown on the TV screens in the bar and yet he still felt the need to say this to me. Some people have found it hard to understand why the jam night was not cancelled that night, considering the news, but I think we all know that if we had cancelled the jam then the terrorists would have won. And nothing sticks it to them more, in my opinion, than a good old-fashioned disco beat. So in many ways, I had done the right thing.

Reunion

When I was sixteen I was walking through Kettering town centre and bumped into a guy called Darren. Darren was a few years above me in school and had been a roadie on the school band trip to Holland two years ago.

'I'm organising a Holland reunion, are you in? We're doing it in Derby because Mr Logan lives in York now and Derby is in between York and Kettering. Are you in? We leave on Saturday morning from the school car park at ten. Are you in?'

I was in. Anything to get back with the old school band crew again; that tour had been one of the happiest weeks of my life. I couldn't wait to sit around with the old gang and reminisce about the bobsled rollercoaster and the parrot soup saga, each of us taking it in turns to do an impression of that guy saying 'parrot soup', speculating between ourselves about where the parrot really did go at six every night. I couldn't wait.

Ten a.m. on Saturday I arrived at the school car park and saw Darren waiting by his car. 'Yes! Second one here!' I crowed.

Darren shook his head, 'Last one here, mate, get in the car, let's go.'

While Darren and I were driving to Derby he explained to me that everybody else, all sixty of them, had RSVP'd 'no' and the Holland reunion was just going to be the two of us plus our ex-teacher Mr Logan hitting the town in Derby (aka Fun Central). I didn't know either of them very well and had never really 'hit the town' before so this would be very interesting, and by interesting I mean scary, uncomfortable and heavily laced with regret. I was never one of those students who thought it was great to see their teachers outside of school in their normal clothes living a normal life like a normal person. I actually preferred to keep them as they were, smartly dressed and in charge, maybe even as role models. What I definitely did not want to do was see them get smashed in Derby town centre, smiling at women then getting pissy when the women didn't smile back, reminding me that none of the adults in my life really know what they're doing and that I too will never fully figure anything out. Luckily, I never fully respected Mr Logan in the first place so this might not be so bad.

Darren and I arrived at the hotel hours before Mr Logan's ETA and headed straight to our room. England were playing Greece at football on the TV. I don't follow football but Darren told me this was a very important game and that as long as England didn't lose then they would qualify for the World Cup. Darren then produced a bottle of peach schnapps from his bag and insisted that every time any of the commentators said 'Beckham' we had to do a shot. Beckham was team captain at the time, was heavily involved in the game and scored the goal that won the match. To be honest, I don't think the commentators said anything other than 'Beckham' for the entire game.

By the end of the game I was a lifeless wreck and felt like I was gonna vom. Peach schnapps is a pretty sickly drink to start the night with, let alone to get fully drunk on, and to this day I can't hear someone say 'Beckham' without wanting to chuck my guts up. Darren went to the pub next door to carry on drinking. I instead chose to have a nap (or a schnap as I would've called it had I possessed the ability to form thoughts and ideas).

I was awoken from my schnap by a loud knocking. I answered the hotel room door, still drunk on schnapps, and did not recognise the man standing, grinning, before me. Mr Logan laughed his head off, chucked his bags in the room, and then took me to the pub where Darren had been drinking solo for about an hour. I didn't much want to be there any more and desperately wanted to feel normal again so I asked for a soft drink and an ice cream sundae and sat very still eating the sundae very slowly while Logan and Darren hit the bar. Schnapps followed by a soft drink and an ice cream sundae called Totally Chocoriffic is something I would never do these days because I know a thing or two about blood sugar, but back then my answer to everything was ice cream. (It still is but I have to pick my moments. I once cheered myself up after a break-up by eating a whole tub of Ben & Jerry's while scrolling down the Ben & Jerry's website reading about the Ben & Jerry's flavours America have that we don't. I would now like a free crate of Ben & Jerry's please.) By the time we left and headed for the town I was sober and riding the dizziest sugar high imaginable while my associates were now thoroughly hammered. I then spent the evening watching two people I didn't know very well get utterly blasted for five hours.

I didn't start properly getting drunk with friends until I was about twenty-three years old and I think the reason I started joining in was because I couldn't stand around watching people getting drunk any more. Not because I was jealous but because when you see people get drunk it looks like the most pointless activity you could ever imagine. You are watching someone become progressively worse as the night goes on and yet they insist it's the best. Unless you also have some sort of buzz going, drunk people are the most irritating company you could ever wish to keep. Having a conversation with a drunk person when you are sober is like being a classroom assistant in a primary school for kids who are drunk.

I was awoken by both Mr Logan and Darren. They were leaning over me, smiling excitedly as they giddily informed me that we would now be trashing the hotel room. I had been woken up to better news in my lifetime. When I was a child I remember my mother waking me up and telling me it was snowing and so I rushed to the window and watched it snow and the world looked pristine and pure and I felt glad to be awake and experiencing life.

When I was told we were trashing the hotel room by an ex-teacher and an older boy I didn't know that well, I immediately started looking forward to twelve hours' time when I could go back to sleep again and put this day behind me, even though none of it had happened yet. I don't know if you've ever trashed a hotel room with your ex-schoolteacher but it's a melancholy activity to say the least. I felt ever so forlorn and yet adrenalin was coursing through my veins all the same. My two accomplices were flipping over mattresses and pushing over lamps, taking their frustrations with the world out on the furniture (and the cleaner, who would inevitably have to deal with the mayhem they had caused).

My only contribution to the room-trashing was to open all the little milks. I didn't even tip them out or splat them against the wall; I just opened them all one by one and arranged them on the table in a line. Those milks were now unusable, I was officially a rebel, the aforementioned cleaner would have to pour them down the sink now, and I had finally become the child my parents always feared I would be – a tearaway of the highest order.

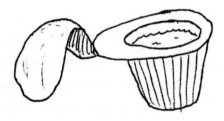

An open milk

Mr Logan, a secondary schoolteacher in his late thirties, emptied the bin into the bath and then left to play golf with some colleagues in York. Darren and I got in his car, turned on Classic FM (the eeriest station to listen to after a hotel room trashing – he put it on as a joke but it still felt like the move of a psychopath) and travelled back to Kettering. In all the excitement of trashing the room I had completely forgotten to brush my teeth so instantly started brushing my teeth in the car while we were driving home on the motorway because if I don't brush my teeth I imagine them coated in fur in my mouth and feel a compulsive need to clean them. But I had not planned ahead, so once I had finished brushing I had no idea where I was supposed to spit. Naturally, I wound down the window and spat out of the window without giving it a second thought. We were travelling at eighty miles per hour so inevitably this resulted in the side of Darren's car getting completely peppered with my toothpaste spit, like a gross minty racing stripe. It had been quite the reunion.

Road Sign

Trashing the hotel room had been my very first act of rebellion. This was because I was a good boy who thought his parents were cool. Shortly after the Holland reunion I attempted to be rebellious once more, but this time out of choice.

I was seventeen, had just left school, and my friend Martin had recently passed his driving test and got his own car. From then on he and I and our friends Stan and Wardy could finally do as we pleased. When the first person in your friendship group gets their driving licence a whole new world opens up for you, a world of infinite possibility – we were free. And so we would regularly get an atlas (already a sign that we're not being as radical as we could be), pick a place in the county we hadn't been before (always within the county as we all had to be home in time for tea), and then we'd drive there. Our destination would usually be a village and once we'd arrived we would walk around said village commenting on how lovely the village was. If you saw me walking round one of these villages admiring a quaint thatched cottage you would never guess I was the same hoodlum who once opened all the milks and left them out on the side.

It may or may not have been pointed out to us by several people that we were an undeniable bunch of dweebs, and so one night we set out to do something well and truly naughty, just because we'd never been well and truly naughty before. We decided that we would steal a road sign. Not a temporary fold-out one, but a permanent, bolted-to-a-pole road sign (the sort that people needed in order to navigate home in the dead of night or during a storm, for example). So we gathered the necessary tools (which Wardy already owned because he was old before his time) and set off at one in the morning, looking for a sign to steal.

It's hard trying to be well and truly naughty when you're not used to being well and truly naughty. Every sign we saw seemed to be a little too important, like if we stole it we might properly ruin someone's life, and so we decided to steal a sign that no one would really miss. We settled on one of those circular blue signs of a person walking and a bicycle underneath them. I believe these signs indicate that a path is for pedestrians *and* cyclists, so that way we were messing with *two* groups of people.

We found a cycle/foot-path by the side of the road that featured one of these signs every few feet, which meant if we stole one we would be inconveniencing no one because they were literally everywhere. The worst thing that *might've* happened is that some pedestrian might one day be walking along that path and a cyclist

'This is a footpath & a cyclepath'

overtakes them at the exact place where the road sign we stole should've been and the pedestrian shouts their complaints after the cyclist, then a few feet later sees a road sign informing them that this is a path for pedestrians and cyclists, at which point they realise it was fine for the cyclist to use the path and then they feel a bit silly for getting cross. Already we were not rebelling against anyone; if anything we were creating an unnecessary job for ourselves when we could've been doing something fun like watching a documentary and then having a discussion about some of the issues it raised.

Oh, and we also decided to film ourselves stealing this sign. This was before the days of camera phones so we had to bring an actual camcorder out with us to film on. We always took this camcorder out with us whenever we went for a drive and until then it had only ever contained footage of lovely villages and charming countryside walks, but now we were using it to film us doing something illegal because that's what well-behaved criminals do – they provide their own evidence so as not to waste anyone's time should things go to trial.

We parked the car next to the path and I set the camcorder to night vision. I was the camera man, Martin the getaway driver, and Stan and Wardy would be stealing the sign. I knelt by the car, filming the whole thing in glorious green. I captured everything, including Wardy mistaking a passing vehicle for a police car, running away and falling into a ditch within seconds. (We considered sending the footage of Wardy falling into the ditch to *You've Been Framed* but didn't for fear of arrest in case the producers watched the rest of the tape and witnessed our dastardly crime. If Beadle had passed the recording on to the po-po we'd have been toast for sure. Getting on *You've Been Framed* wouldn't make up for a lifetime in the clink and we probably couldn't bail all four of us out with the £250 they paid us either.)

Wardy clambered out of the ditch and finished the theft. Credit where it's due, they took down the road sign rather efficiently, as is the way when you're usually a well-behaved group of boys – you tend to be quite good at organising and planning and getting the job done smoothly. We'd already foreseen any potential hitches and had dealt with them all accordingly. When we watched the footage back, the moment where they managed to separate the sign from the pole was both exhilarating and pathetic. Wardy and Stan remove the sign, excitedly shout, 'We've got it, oh my god, we've got it!' then all three of us run back into the car, squealing with glee, the doors slamming behind us. Then we all cheer and Martin presses play on the stereo and

'Movies' by the band Alien Ant Farm blasts out of the speakers at full volume as we all drive off singing along to it and passing the sign between us, laughing like maniacs.

At that moment I felt immortal. I can try and play it down but that would be dishonest. It was intoxicating. I would whole-heartedly recommend stealing a road sign that no one really needs because then you too will know how it feels to be alive. In fact, any chance you get to do something technically illegal while making zero difference to anyone's life, take it. I know, I know, I'm an appalling role model and yes, if everyone stole one of those cycle/foot-path signs then it would end up affecting people because there'd be no signs letting people know if it's OK to cycle and walk on the same path but I think after maybe half of them go missing the police will crack down on it, so if you are planning on stealing one of these signs my advice is get in early before the fuzz have got their peepers all over them.

Wardy kept the sign in his room. The pigs never caught us. Wardy's mum did see it on his shelf one day and asked what it was doing in his room so, without putting up much of a fight, he 'fessed up and told her everything. Once he'd finished singing like a canary she looked disappointed but not in the way he'd hoped for. We all ended up telling our parents and receiving the same reaction. What's a guy got to do to get told off these days? The last time I'd received a proper dressing-down was when I used Siobhan's coat as my own personal towel. Did I have to go back to school in order to ever get in trouble again?! As it turned out, yes, that's precisely what I was supposed to do.

Shortcut

Back when I was in secondary school I would often walk from my house to my friend George's house and cut through the school grounds to get there. Even on the weekends or after school hours it was easy to make this shortcut. I would leave my parents' house, walk to the school, continue through the main entrance, cut diagonally across the playground and then across the big playing field, walk through the gap in the hedge and then I'd be on the street adjacent to George's. It shaved about half an hour off the journey. Great shortcut.

When I left school I carried on doing this. This was the late nineties, early 00s and there was nothing to stop anyone who wanted to from walking on to school property whenever they wanted. Plus the staff at my school liked it when old students returned to say hello and I would often combine the shortcut with a quick catch-up with one of my old teachers. Great shortcut. Then I didn't do it for a few months because I'd learned to drive (more on that later).

I left school at seventeen and went to college in Northampton to take a BTEC Music course. While at the college I had met a group of musicians and joined a band called The New Hardcore Skiffle Movement (this band would later go on to be known as Three Line Whip). All was well.

And then one fine day when I was nineteen-ish, I decided to pay a visit to my buddy George, and since it was such a beautiful day I thought it'd be nice to do the old walk again. As I approached the school I noticed that there was a very high fence surrounding the building. *That's new,* I thought to myself, but the main entrance to the school was still wide open and so I walked in as always. It was one o'clock so I knew all the students would be in their lessons and I could cut across in peace. But as soon as my feet touched the playground tarmac, an alarm went off. Not in my head, I mean a literal alarm, really loud and ringing throughout the entire school. Had my school installed a security system whereby if someone from outside steps on to school property it triggers an alarm? I hoped not, as I was sure they would all feel very silly when they realised it was me, James Acaster, the best student that ever attended this fine institution and not some sinister stranger one would usually need to sound an alarm for. But I soon learnt that it wasn't an alarm, it was the lunch bell.

It turned out that lunchtime (which should always be at midday) had been pushed back a whole hour since my day and so within seconds the playground was flooded with secondary school kids. The kids were running round, playing games, and looking at the unfamiliar adult who shouldn't be there and was standing, bemused, in the middle of their tennis court. At that moment a dinner lady walked up to me. I hadn't met her before so she must've been new and therefore perhaps wasn't coming over to chat about old times.

'Can I help you?' she asked.

'No thanks,' I replied coolly, 'I'm just cutting through.'

She looked puzzled. 'Well you can't do that.'

This was news to me as I'd been doing just that for years and no one had minded. But as soon as she said, 'You can't do that,' it sort of made instant sense and sounded beyond reasonable.

'You're going to have to leave,' she said, which also sounded totally fair. I had no problem with leaving as that had been my plan all along. When you're taking a shortcut through somewhere, your only plan is to leave that place; I was never going to hang around for a while.

'Will do,' I said and began to continue on my way.

'No, back the way you came,' she said sternly.

'But the distance is the same,' I pleaded. 'Can't I just carry on this way?'

Her patience was wearing thin. 'If you want to go that way and continue to be on school premises you'll have to sign in,' she stated, and pointed towards the reception area. And so in my stubbornness I decided that signing in was exactly what I'd do.

The main reason I chose to sign in was because I felt like I was beginning to look like a suspicious character and I wanted to prove beyond a shadow of a doubt that I was anything but a suspicious character. One thing a suspicious character would never do is sign in, and so by signing in I was demonstrating how much the opposite of suspicious I was. I walked into the reception area and up to the reception desk where a receptionist was dealing with someone else. There was a sign-in sheet on a clipboard on the desk so I started to fill it out.

'Name' was easy enough (James Acaster). 'Reason For Visit' was easy too (cutting through). But 'Time In' and 'Time Out' kind of threw me as I would be leaving straight away so those times would both technically be the same and I wasn't sure if you were allowed to put the same time for 'Time In' and 'Time Out'. As I stared at the sheet the receptionist asked if I needed a hand and so, like an idiot, I explained my problem to her.

'I'm just cutting through the school on my way to George's house and so I'm a little unsure if it's OK to just put the same time for "Time In" and "Time Out".'

She looked at me the way most people look at someone who's just said something offensively ludicrous and then took the clipboard away from me. 'You're cutting through?'

'Yes, I'm on my way to George's house but I'm not sure if I should just put the same time for "Time In" *and* "Time Out", you see.'

Her expression didn't change. 'We're a school, not a public footpath.'

'Yeah but I used to go here, it's fine, it's fine! I'm James Acaster, it's fine!'

It wasn't fine. She put the clipboard behind the desk and walked to the door. 'I'm getting the deputy head.'

She left the room and I sat down in the waiting area. I had been back in school for five seconds and I was already in trouble with the deputy head. I sat there waiting for Mr Barley to turn up so I could finally explain myself to someone who knew me and knew I wasn't a bad egg. Mr Barley liked me, always had. I worked very hard in his maths classes and he helped me pass my maths GCSE. Yeah, me and Old Barley would sort all this out. Once Barley arrived we'd have a ruddy good catch-up; he'd probably get me to recreate the Eco Man sketch right there in the reception area, and perhaps a rendition of 'La La La Humpty' for old time's sake. This receptionist was going to look like quite the fool once Barley arrived and told her she was currently delaying the drummer and founding member of Pindrop.

As you've probably guessed, Mr Barley had retired and instead I got some other guy I'd never met before. He was tall and well built. I mean, he looked *tough*, bald-headed and angry that this little punk was trying to cut through his school. I tried to explain to him that I used to go to the school, that there must be plenty of teachers in the staffroom who could vouch for me, but he wasn't having any of it – I had to leave. I agreed that leaving was a good idea but again asked if I could just continue the way I was going. This man was very angry and getting angrier by the second. He told me I would leave the school the way I came and that he didn't want to hear another word about it. Even though he was turning a furious shade of red I was still eerily relaxed about the whole thing. The reason I was still so relaxed is because I had tried to cut through the school during mufti day and the deputy head was now bollocking me while wearing a Hawaiian shirt and shorts. You can't take anyone seriously when they're dressed for a day of chilling on the beach. He should've been holding a pina colada and rubbing sun tan lotion all over his bald head while telling me off.

But even so, I did as I was told and left the premises. I may not have succeeded at breaking any rules since I left school but it was nice to know that back on my old stomping ground I was once again considered a troublesome rebel.

Fiesta

As I mentioned in the previous story, I had now learnt to drive. The only reason I had 'chosen' to walk to George's house that day was because eight days after I passed my driving test, I had written off my parents' Ford Fiesta and didn't drive for a while after that. Before I tell this story it's important that you know that no one was hurt. Also, this is the first of three stories in this book (a trilogy, yes) where I write off a car. Because I have written off three cars.

Ok, cool, here we go.

I was eighteen and had gone out to meet some friends for the night. We met up in a pub but none of us drank any alcohol because we were all driving and we were good boys (you are correct in assuming it was the same boys I stole the road sign with).

When you're eighteen and you've just passed your driving test and you're driving home on your own late at night, you tend to feel pretty carefree. And maybe drive a little bit faster than you should. And maybe go round a corner where there's mud on the road and lose control of the car.

The car skidded and span, everything moved way too fast for me to even figure out what was happening or what I should do to stop it carrying on. I hadn't been taught how to deal with this during my lessons, I had only been taught how to prevent it from happening in the first place, but seeing as I had chosen to ignore that advice the moment I got my driver's licence, I was now in a spot of bother.

The car came off the road and over quite a high grass verge; this caused the car to bounce up and down clumsily. At one point the car bounced sideways into a hedge then back on to the verge then back into the hedge then back on to the verge then back into a hedge and then on to the verge. I felt like I was inside a pinball machine. The final time the car hit the grass verge it landed on the two wheels on the right hand side and then balanced on those two wheels at a precarious angle. I knew that if the car fell on its roof something bad could happen because the car was small, it wasn't moving fast enough to roll and instead it would just slam into the ground. I sat and waited, my head touching the ceiling, while the car gently rocked, making up its mind which way to fall, and then eventually landed on all four wheels again.

I then said out loud, 'Shit, I've just crashed the car.' That's what I like to do when something scary happens and I'm on my own, I just confirm it with myself and swear at the start so I never forget that I am a badass.

Even though I had openly acknowledged the fact I had definitely crashed the car, I still tried to drive away. If you've ever crashed a car you'll know that you don't want to accept it, running immediately into the arms of denial. I thought maybe I could drive home and my parents would never need to know what happened. To my utter relief the car started and I drove off. And then the car stalled two seconds later and lay dead and unmoving in the middle of the road. I tried to start it again but it showed no sign of life. I tried to turn the lights on – also nothing. And then I saw the headlights of another car coming towards me, fast. I looked in the rear view mirror and saw another set of headlights approaching even faster from behind. Then both cars reached me at the exact same time, saw my car at the very last second, swerved around me and ended up hitting each other.

Once again I feel like I should point out, everyone was fine.

In the short-term anyway.

I may have gone a little off the rails for about six months...

Skydive

After writing off my parents' Fiesta I had myself a midlife crisis (yes at eighteen). I was terrified I wasn't doing enough with my life and that one day there was even a chance I would be dead. I had not seen the film *The Bucket List*, it hadn't even been released at the time, but I decided there were a few things I simply had to experience before death and so made a list of those things (what I'm saying is, I came up with the idea for *The Bucket List* before it even came out). There were three things on the list that I managed to achieve. One was to try stand-up comedy, which I initially put off out of fear. Another was to do volunteer work which was much easier as I knew someone who worked at the Kettering Volunteer Bureau (obviously I always referred to this as 'The Bureau' so I could feel like a cool FBI guy whenever I went in there). They sent me to paint an elderly woman's kitchen − something I actually had no experience of, and so I did what is commonly referred to as a hideous job. Her kitchen somehow looked worse than it did before I painted it, getting progressively worse the more work I did on it. Quite remarkable.

After making a sweet old lady's kitchen look unbearably ugly I was asked by The Bureau if there was anything they could do for me in return. Because I felt guilty about the kitchen I tried to think of the one thing on my do-before-I-die list that they wouldn't be able to help me with so I said I'd like to try stand-up comedy. To my relief they said they didn't really do that sort of stuff and sent me on my way.

Then two days later they rang me saying that a guy had come into The Bureau asking for help setting up a stand-up comedy workshop in Kettering and so they had put my name down to attend since they already knew I was keen. There was one workshop a week for nine weeks and three of us attended. Our teacher would always be drinking a pack of beers and he never strictly taught us anything, but I think that was actually a good thing. Every week he'd just make us get up one by one and do ten minutes of new material to the other three people in the room and then he'd either say, 'That was funny' or 'That was shit'. I honestly think that this is the best way to help someone get started in stand-up − no instruction, no tips, just make them start. Put them in a position where they're forced to figure it out by themselves and at the end of it all put them on stage and make them do a gig.

The guy who ran the workshop was called Jim Watts and on the night of our first gig he told us we were setting ourselves apart from 99.9 per cent of the population just by getting on stage, so it didn't matter how it went. I still remind myself of this fact every time I've just been unfunny on stage. That first gig was in a local pub in Kettering. It was fun and went better than I expected but I didn't consider moving into it as a career because Three Line Whip was still going strong and I was going to be an extremely influential musician/genius. So for the next couple of years I would do a comedy gig once every four months just because I enjoyed it.

One of the other goals on the I'm-going-to-die list was to do a skydive.

I saw a poster advertising the chance to do a charity skydive and it felt perfect. I would get to fulfill a life goal while raising money for something, thus making myself feel like a good person in the process. The charity was Age Concern, quite fitting when you consider I was currently fretting over my own mortality. If anyone was concerned about ageing it was James Acaster, so in a way I was raising money for myself – win-win. Having said that, if I was truly concerned about the aged I'd probably have taken more care when painting their kitchens. It turns out it's actually not easy to get people to donate to Age Concern because the name doesn't sound urgent enough. Very few charities reel people in by playing on their concern. I would tell people I was collecting for Age Concern and they would look baffled and ask, 'Well, what's wrong with them? Why the concern?' to which I would answer, 'They're old.' If it was called Age Crisis I'd have raised some big bucks in next to no time. There is a world of difference between crisis and concern, that's all I'm saying. Anyway it's a great charity; please give what you can.

Once I had raised enough money I assumed doing the actual skydive would be fairly simple. However, I had a bunch of jumps cancelled for various reasons:

Jump One – too cloudy. We got all the way up to 12,000 feet in the plane and then just flew back down again and went home. You would think they'd be able to tell how cloudy it is from the ground; I still don't know why we had to go all the way up there in the plane to figure out that there were clouds in the sky.

Rescheduled Jump – too cloudy. Couldn't we just jump through the clouds though, really? It's not like we're going to hit any clouds on the way down, guys!! It was safe enough to fly up here so surely it's safe enough to jump down again!!

Rescheduled Rescheduled Jump – another skydiver messed up his landing and slipped a disc in his back and so no one else could jump that day because he was lying in the landing zone waiting for the ambulance in agony. He messed up his landing because it was too cloudy and he couldn't see where he was going (I'm guessing).

So when I arrived at the airfield to do the rescheduled rescheduled rescheduled jump I was extremely laid-back, because as far as I was concerned I would once again end up not jumping out of a plane that day. I skipped the safety course (I'd done it three times and knew it back to front), absolutely destroyed a child at big Jenga in the waiting room, watched an episode of *Friends* and then, two hours later, they called my name along with a bunch of other people and we got into the plane. I talked to everyone on the plane like I hadn't a care in the world, knowing that something would once again get in the way and stop me from doing the jump. But on this particular day nothing got in the way at all and so I ended up jumping out of a plane without having prepared myself for jumping out of a plane. I wasn't prepared mentally, emotionally or physically, and so it ended up feeling like I had been unexpectedly pushed out of a plane for real.

Just so I don't put you off entirely I should mention that the free fall element of skydiving is incredible and I loved it. Before the parachute opened and after I had accepted the fact that I was about to die, it was an experience like no other and that alone made the whole thing worth it. To my surprise, my skydiving instructor loved the experience even more than I did, he was whooping and shrieking in a way that led me to believe this was his first time too and maybe they had accidentally attached two newbies together and pushed us out of the plane without realising, and meanwhile two professional instructors were attached to one another, free-falling in silence and each wondering why the other wasn't more excited.

'Woooooooo! Yeah! How do you like free fall, James?!?!?!,' he screamed in my ear.

'It's good,' I said. After we'd been free-falling for a while he pulled the chord and released the parachute, which meant we got pulled sharply from a horizontal position to a standing position and my stomach went haywire.

'Check this out, James!' he hollered, before steering the parachute left and right, zig-zagging across the sky, my stomach always trailing a few feet behind us, failing to catch up with the rest of my body. Without a shadow of a doubt I was going to chuck up if he carried on like this – if he'd said the word 'Beckham' then that would've sealed it and I would've erupted.

'Sorry, mate, do you think we could not move around as much? I'm feeling queasy.' I have never found out for sure but I think 'queasy' is the word that skydivers hate the most. This guy had been fairly quiet in the plane. He had just sat there, moodily staring out the window, no interest in conversation, but then sprang into life once we jumped. It was like he had transformed into a bird and was finally free. But now I was raining on his parade and had dropped the Q-word. He immediately started sulking.

'Fine,' he said and we stopped zagging. We just drifted silently and slowly in a general downwards direction. I couldn't see his face because he was behind me but could sense his disappointment. Every time he exhaled he'd huff loudly in my ear like a stroppy teenager. We were still incredibly high up at this point and moving very slowly, which made me start to panic even more. I kept all the panic internal but I felt like I was going to be sick and didn't want to start being sick while trapped in the sky, I wanted to do it in a lovely toilet on the ground. Then another problem arose and this one was definitely my fault.

If there's one piece of advice I would give anyone doing a skydive it would be this – do not under any circumstance wear slip-ons. Wear shoes with shoelaces that will stay on your feet no matter what because you are about to fall through the sky and that's where all the wind lives. As we floated around aimlessly and my skydiving instructor's eyes burned into the top of my head, one of my slip-ons began to slip off (the exact opposite of what I'd bought the slip-on for). I couldn't tell him because I was certain he would instantly unclip me and let me fall to my thoroughly deserved death. But I really, really didn't want my slip-on to fall thousands of feet and embed itself in a cow's brain because that was without question what I believed would happen if I didn't keep it on my foot. In order to stop this from happening I had to curl my toes up towards my shins and hold them in that position all the way down, thus hooking the slip-on with my foot.

Skydiving

It took so long for us to reach the ground. We were drifting for what felt like an eternity, plus it was super uncomfortable and made me panic even more about being sick because if I was sick there was no way I'd be able to keep the slip-on on my foot in the process and so I would be dropping vomit and footwear at the same time and it would look like I had hurled up a slip-on and everyone would think I eat shoes whole and then have the nerve to complain about feeling 'queasy' when eating shoes doesn't agree with me.

By the time we came in to land I felt terribly faint. 'You won't be able to do the landing we practised because you're feeling so poorly, so we're going to have to do an emergency landing,' the instructor said to me. *Oh great, I'm slipping a disc, that's what's happening now*, I thought. *Just like that man last time, I'll slip a disc and then the ambulance will take an hour to arrive and no one else will be able to jump because I'm a big wimp with a slipped disc. Here we go, get ready to slip a disc, James, that's what's about to happen to you – disc-slipping time. First your slip-on slips off and now your disc is about to do the same. Congratulations. That's you, slipping all over the shop, king of the slips, say goodbye to your disc you slippy embarrassment.*

As we came in to land he started yelling to the people below, 'We've got a sleeper! We've got a sleeper!' Which sounds an awful lot like 'We've got a slipper!' I initially panicked thinking that he had just confirmed my biggest fear and that I was unavoidably about to slip a disc, or maybe my slip-on had slipped off without my knowledge and he was warning the crowd of the incoming missile, but fortunately he shouted, 'We've got a sleeper' about ten more times and so I quickly figured out that I wasn't a Slipper I was a Sleeper.

Everyone always learns something about themselves when doing extreme things like skydiving and I had learned that I was a Sleeper, which isn't an ideal thing to be when jumping out of a plane – asleep. He shouted it so loudly as well, which was irksome as I didn't want everybody to know I was a Sleeper, I wanted it to be a secret. And so everyone watched as the Sleeper rolled into town, a single limp slip-on hanging off his foot, not doing the same landing as everyone else where the instructor and the pupil both lift their legs up at the same time and land safely on the ground, all smooth and cool. The Sleeper and his angry friend had to resort instead to skidding along the ground on their butts like a couple of twonks, a couple of twonks who hated each other and would never ever speak to each other again.

As I lay on my back, my instructor patiently laying underneath me because he was unable to get up until I got up, someone ran over and took our photograph. Later on, my mum bought that photograph for five pounds. I look like I've completely passed out in the photo and my instructor is looking off camera at some of his mates with a look on his face that says, 'Why is it always me?' The photo is still on display in my parents' house and serves as a reminder that, while I will die one day, there are some things that are way worse than dying and it's important to experience those things while we're alive in order to put death into perspective; that way we won't get too down about our own mortality.

Porcelain

The skydive was one of the few things I had achieved on the list and during the daytime, when Three Line Whip didn't have band practice, I was so bored. No matter how hard I worked on the band I always found myself with a lot of spare time, and with my new found fear of dying I was now trying to fill that time up with anything I could. Any opportunity to feel like I wasn't wasting what precious little time I had on this earth, sign me up.

The best example of this was the time my parents, who had never shown an interest in French porcelain, inexplicably received an invitation in the post to attend a French porcelain exhibition. I asked them if they were going to accept the invitation and they said no, because they didn't like porcelain exhibitions, plus they had no idea why they'd been invited in the first place, and so I asked if I could go in their place and they said yes, because who cares. I think I imagined some grand exhibition, the finest French porcelain on display for only a select few to see, like the opening of a prestigious art gallery. But since it's made it into this book you can probably guess it was nothing like that.

The exhibition was taking place at a nearby hotel. I arrived on time, handed my invitation in at reception and they took me into a waiting room with the other attendees. I was the youngest one there by about fifty years. Everyone else was real old, the kind of age that might even elicit some 'concern', maybe inspire people to raise some money for them in order to alleviate some of that concern, perhaps by means of a skydive, who's to say? There were twenty of us in total and we waited patiently while drinking free cups of tea, in silence. There was a buffet but no one had touched it yet so I too resisted and waited patiently. The door to the main exhibition room opened (in my memory the door opened on its own) and a French man's voice from inside boomed, 'Enter!'

We filtered timidly into the room, which was was huge but virtually empty. At the far end was a long table, behind the table was a tall shelving unit full of porcelain, and behind that was a partition.

'Please approach the table!' boomed the voice. And so we all spread out along one side of the empty table, looking across at the porcelain with intrigue and suspicion.

A tall, broad-shouldered man in an expensive suit appeared from behind the partition, then walked around so he was standing in front of the shelves and behind the table. He spread his arms wide as he introduced himself.

'My name is Michelle!' he announced. Now obviously that's not how his name is spelt but it's how it's pronounced and it caused one of the old men to let out a loud, high-pitched laugh, which ended abruptly when his wife jabbed him sharply in the ribs. Michel probably knew at this point that this was going to be a tough gig.

He then proceeded to tell us that he represented one of the most respected porcelain companies in the entire world and that we were the very lucky few that had been selected to attend this exclusive event. He also revealed that one of us would be walking away with over five thousand pounds' worth of French porcelain for free. The old people looked at each other in disbelief; they were clearly thrilled. None of us knew what we had to do in order to win the porcelain yet, but being the youngest by some distance I was crossing my fingers for some sort of physical challenge, maybe a Royal Rumble, so I could walk my way to an easy victory. I may have been throwing myself out of a plane for these people a matter of weeks ago but I would trample every last one of them into the ground if it meant walking away with some free crockery from our friends across the Channel.

Michel then walked back behind the partition and stayed there for the rest of the presentation. He was taller than the partition so had to crouch the whole time with his hands on his knees. His job for the remainder of the afternoon appeared to be aggressively shushing the old people whenever they got too excited and started nattering, whilst a lady dressed in a similar suit appeared from the other side of the partition and stood in his place. I hoped *her* name was Michelle but alas, it was Juliette.

Michel crouching behind the partition

Juliette was also French and told us the full history of the company, as well as talking us through every single plate and dish on the shelves. She also explained in detail the reason why each piece of porcelain had a different plant painted on it. (Not that I remember the reason now. It was probably because plants look nice when painted on plates.) One dish had a thistle painted on it. Juliette found it difficult to say 'thistle' though and pronounced it 'fiffle'. This resulted in one of the most bizarre yet beautiful moments I've ever been fortunate enough to witness.

Juliette said, 'And this is a fiffle,' and then all of the old people went, 'No, no, it's a thistle!'

So Juliette tried again. 'Fiffle?'

'No, thistle!'

'Fiffle?'

'Thistle!'

'Fiffle?'

'Thistle!'

'Fiffle?'

'Thistle!'

'Fiffle?'

'Thistle!'

'Fiffle?'

'Thistle!'

'Fiffle?'

'Thistle!'

'Fiffle?'

'Thistle!'

I'll cut this short but it went on for longer than I ever dreamed it could have and neither side altered what they were saying. It was Parrot Soup all over again. After a while I began to prefer 'fiffle' and decided to start saying it like that all the time, even though I knew it was wrong, in the hope that people would always correct me so I could go through the fiffle/thistle rigmarole again and again.

Juliette soon regained the higher ground, however, when she passed a plate to one of the old ladies and asked her what would be the first thing she would do with the plate once she'd taken it down from the shelves in her home, and the old lady paused, panicked, and mimed licking the plate. Even as she mimed the single lick across the diameter of the plate, holding it in two hands like a squirrel holding a nut, you could see in her eyes that she knew she'd messed up (the correct answer apparently was to look at the back of the plate to check that it bears the official stamp of the company but surely if you owned the porcelain you'd already know the stamp was present and accounted for so why wouldn't you skip the unnecessary inspection and dive straight in for a bit of a lick?). Anyway, that old lady never recovered and looked mortified for the rest of the lecture.

It was now time for Juliette to decide who would walk away with the free porcelain. All we had to do was answer three simple questions by raising our hands.

'Question one! Did you like the porcelain I showed you today?'

We all raised our hands. Question one was such an easy question, I would've been shocked if the correct answer had turned out to be no. She revealed that the correct answer was in fact – yes. No one was eliminated in the first round.

'Question two! Who would like to have some of this porcelain free of charge?'

We all raised our hands. I was confident with question two as well. I was pretty sure that if I wanted to win some free French porcelain and someone asked, 'Who would like some porcelain for free?' that the correct answer was 'Me'. Juliette narrowed her eyes at me and walked over.

'I'll have you knew I am a psychologist and can tell if you are lying,' she said very sternly. I kept my hand raised defiantly and nodded my head. I wasn't lying; I did want the porcelain for free. She had no idea how wrong she was. Bring on the final question.

'Question three! If we give you this porcelain for free would you be prepared to have your initials engraved on the back of every single bit of porcelain, which costs five hundred pounds per initial?'

All of the hands went down except for the plate-licker. I was fairly certain that the correct answer was 'Yes' but I was willing to risk it at this stage and hope that the answer she was looking for was in fact, 'Never in a million years.' I don't know if the plate-licking lady hadn't heard the third question or simply didn't realise she hadn't put her hand down but as we were all told to get out of the room because we were eliminated (Juliette pointed at us all one by one, saying 'eliminated' every time), the plate-licking lady looked very surprised indeed. Just as the door closed behind me, I saw her doing a little victory dance on the spot and I think to this day it's one of the saddest sights I've seen, an old lady doing the twist because she'd just been completely swizzed by a French porcelain saleswoman. I felt sorry for her and I felt worried about what was about to happen to her. It was at this moment that I finally understood the concept of Age Concern. So once again I urge you, give what you can and together we can stop old, plate-licking ladies from falling into the hands of Continental Con-Men.

It was then that me and the rest of the eliminated old people descended upon the buffet. Now we all knew what kind of a racket they were running here, there was no way we weren't going to take full advantage of the free eats (unless we had to pay to have our initials engraved into the back of each sandwich). As we were piling nibbles on to our paper plates (you would've thought they'd have at least provided us with porcelain plates – let us dream a little, we would've given them back after), one of the old ladies said to her husband, 'Oh we should leave some for the lady who won, surely?' and as he stacked up three eclairs against a mini scotch egg and a big pork pie he looked back at the main room and said in a husky voice, like an Everest mountain climber deciding not to go back for one of their party, 'No, love... she knew the risk when she kept her hand up.'

Ice Skating

Even after attending a French porcelain exhibition I somehow still didn't feel like I was living my life to the full, so I decided to get more organised. I came up with the idea of doing a 'new thing' every single night for a week. No one had set me this challenge, I just thought I needed to have some new experiences and broaden my horizons before I would be dead for ever (yes, I was still eighteen at the time.) Initially, this project wasn't something I had planned; it actually started by accident.

It was Monday 13 February and I had a date. And no, the new thing I did that night was not 'go on a date' but hahaha well done. That being said, I was not well versed in dating and I think I'd watched way too many indie romance movies to know that people didn't always enjoy going on dates with someone who's deliberately acting kooky. I picked up my date for the evening (against their better instincts, my parents allowed me to borrow the car for the night, presumably because they hoped I was meeting my future wife) and when she got in the car, I proudly announced that I had got absolutely nothing planned for us whatsoever. At the time I think I thought she'd be impressed by, and attracted to, this guy's spontaneous attitude. Looking back, I can see how I may have come across like I didn't care how the night went or what we got up to, and maybe saying I hadn't bothered to plan anything was an instant turn-off.

So we drove around aimlessly, trying to find somewhere to go. She spotted a sign for an ice rink and so it was decided that we would go ice skating, and I finally understood why most people plan their dates in advance. Spoiler alert – I couldn't ice skate. But I still agreed to go ice-skating because if I said no to her suggestion then that wouldn't exactly fit with my new spontaneous persona. You can't say, 'We'll do whatever we may chance upon this fine evening!' then when someone suggests ice skating say, 'Not that.' I had ice skated once before for only five minutes when I was ten and had to stop because I had managed to stab myself in the back with my own ice skate while I was still wearing it.[3]

I wasn't sure when would be a good time to bring up the fact I couldn't ice skate. She was definitely going to figure it out because at some point I'd have to put ice skates on and go out on the ice and stab myself in the back in front of her. But a part of me hoped that maybe I'd be good at it, maybe I would suddenly

---

3 I still don't understand how I managed this but I was, and still am, very gangly.

be able to ice skate and she need not know that I'd never properly skated before.

On the bright side I've never seen someone laugh as much as she laughed that night. I did that thing when you just walk around the ice and don't technically skate at all. I just walked like a normal person on normal ground and then occasionally would lose my confidence and 'wobble all over the place like a baby giraffe that's just been born' (her words). She lapped me countless times and during the course of the date she mentioned that at the end of the week she would be leaving the UK for a year. I can only hope the trip was something she had planned before the date started.

Because she would be leaving the country, I thought it was best to get another date in quickly so I asked if she was up to anything the following day. She said she was going line dancing and asked me if I'd like to join her and I said yes right away because that's what spontaneous people do. It was only once she'd left the car and I had driven away that I realised that tomorrow was Valentine's Day.

Line Dancing

I was not allowed use of the car the following day and so I had to ask my younger brother Stephen to give me a lift to line dancing. On the way I received a text from my date telling me she would no longer be able to attend because her mum had thrown her a surprise Valentine's Day party, an excuse that I believed at the time, but don't worry, I am now fully aware that I got well and truly swerved. Even though she'd cancelled on me I didn't want to turn round and go home because I had already got myself into the line dancing headspace and I was really looking forward to giving it a go. When I told Stephen this he did the nicest thing he could've done in that situation and offered to accompany me to line dancing instead. I think it's only right that at this point we all take a moment to admire Stephen and what a superb brother he is. He could've cut and run, he could've just taken me home and left it at that, maybe used his evening with the car to go and do something that *he* wanted to do, but he didn't, he committed himself to an evening of dancing in formation to music he didn't even remotely enjoy while someone barked orders at him through a PA system just because his brother had gotten majorly swerved without realising it. What a guy!

The line dancing class was held in a hall in some sort of community centre. Everything was beige and tan. We entered the room and received puzzled stares from the other members of the class, mainly because we were the only people there under the age of fifty. Most of our classmates were in their seventies, all of them were women and none of them were expecting us in the slightest. The leader of the line dancing class was a lady called Dee. I know this because she was wearing a T-shirt that said 'Dee's Devils'. A few of the other ladies were also wearing Dee's Devils T-shirts and some of them had plastic devil horns on their head. Once they'd established we hadn't walked into the wrong room by mistake, they welcomed us to the group and the class began.

First things first, line dancing is stupendous. Steve and I both had a lot of fun. Whenever we were asked to turn to the right or step to the left my brother would slap his thigh like a cowboy and it was funny every single time. Dee was zinging me throughout the night but I didn't even care. At one point someone spilt some water near me and she accused me of wetting myself and everyone laughed at me but I was just as on-board with the joke as the rest of them and laughed louder than anyone else. (Or maybe in my head I did. Actually, it may have taken me a while to figure out what she meant by 'you could've waited,' but I definitely laughed at her joke and suppressed my instinct to defend myself by pointing out that if anyone was going to wet themselves at line dancing, it would be one of the many pensioners in attendance, pensioners who would never laugh at incontinence if it happened to one of their own but absolutely lap it up when the shoe's on the other foot. For shame.)

I am also aware that at this stage in the book it's starting to sound like my social circle mainly consisted of the elderly. The porcelain exhibition, line dancing, painting their kitchens, jumping out of planes to raise money for them – I hadn't realised until writing this book that immediately after the car crash and getting confronted with my own mortality I did suddenly end up gravitating more towards the aged. Maybe I was subconsciously facing my fears head on? Staring death in the face instead of hiding from it? But I was just the sort of teenager who preferred/loved activities usually reserved for people well into their retirement.

At the end of our class Dee said, 'Great work everyone, time for the professionals now, feel free to stay and watch if you want to see some quality line dancing!'

Even though this was a massive kick in the collective guts of the group, it was intriguing enough to make Stephen and I want to stay behind and watch the professionals at work. The professionals, it turned out, were all around the same age as we were, all of them were women and they were all exceptional line dancers. I thought I'd picked up line dancing surprisingly easily until I saw them move at speeds I could only dream of and not one of them laughed when the person next to them slapped their thigh for a joke. (Mainly because no one did slap their thigh for a joke. I have since learnt that slapping your thigh for a joke is frowned upon within the world of professional line dancing.)

Once their class was over, four of the line dancers came over and started to talk to us (with their mother, but still). They asked us how long we'd been line dancing for, how we were enjoying it so far, whether we'd come back next week. They offered to teach Stephen some new moves and took him by the hand over to the dance floor. (From what I could tell they were teaching him Michael Jackson dance moves but I'm not certain. Does Michael Jackson count as line dancing?) Their mum stayed with me and carried on chatting. We talked about dancing and her son who was a professional dancer named Hypno. Hypno would often begin his routines in the foetal position and then pop and lock his way out of an imaginary womb, as if he were being born. I looked over at Stephen who was being taught a dance move where you look like you're pushing your own body parts around with your hand, and thought, *Considering I got cancelled on tonight, this has actually worked out pretty well. Four ladies our age are hanging out with us and we're having fun.* I could feel my ego healing itself. Then the mother pointed at Stephen and asked me, 'So how long have you been together?'

On the way home I thought it best not to tell Stephen that the ladies who'd been paying him so much attention didn't really fancy either one of us and they actually thought we were a sweet couple going line dancing together for Valentine's. He'd had a good night and there was no need to take that away from him just yet. I did tell him the very next morning and he took it rather well. If anything, learning the truth helped him make sense of the previous evening and why we had suddenly become babe magnets. Sometimes it's nice to confirm that the world is exactly as you thought it was and your role in it remains entirely the same.

Karaoke

When I got home from line dancing, it occurred to me that I had spent two nights in a row doing things that were outside of my comfort zone so I decided to try and maintain that for a week because I was bored and I had enjoyed line dancing far more than I thought I was going to and also because I was going to be dead one day.

The next day I went online and searched, 'Things to do on a Wednesday night in Kettering' – the internet gave me nothing. This is typical. Things happen to you when you're not looking for them and as soon as you try to make them happen again you can't. The only thing that came up after a lot of delving was a karaoke night in a village nearby. This would definitely be a new experience for me as I had avoided singing in public, especially at karaoke nights, pretty much all my life. I had not sung in public since 'La La La Humpty' and before that I had bailed on my solo in the St Andrew's Primary School production of *The Woodcutter and the Christmas Dove*. I had clearly been very nervous about singing as a child and then when I finally did sing in front of my class in secondary school, I was made to do it over and over again until it wasn't fun any more. This is the reason why I avoided singing in Pindrop and we ended up with a singer who may or may not have been a double agent working for another band who'd sent him on a mission to sabotage us at every turn. It was time to put all that behind me though; I couldn't be scared any more. Maybe I'd freeze up, maybe I'd be so good they'd make me come back every week to perform for them until I retired on stage. Regardless of the outcome it felt important to try.

At the time I could think of nothing I'd prefer less than singing karaoke in public but if I didn't give it a go then this new project of mine would be over before it'd even begun. And so I drove to the pub in question completely alone. I hadn't invited anyone to come with me because I didn't want any of my friends to see me singing but as soon as I arrived at the pub and saw people singing karaoke in front of their mates I realised that singing alone with no support whatsoever in front of a room of judgmental strangers who weren't obligated to get behind me with cheers of encouragement was actually worse. I really, really did not want to do it and what's more nobody was forcing me to in the slightest – just me and the rules I had set myself for no reason. Despite all of this, I still approached the guy in charge and put my name down on the list. The song I chose to sing in front of a pub full of strangers was 'Every Little Thing She Does

Is Magic' by The Police. I think singing a song like that when you've turned up on your own and no one is cheering you on is actually sadder than singing a Smiths song or some other depressing number. Tragic, in fact. Merrily singing about a woman who lights up your life and makes everything worth it, while quite clearly on my own with no one standing beside me is as bleak as it gets. Let's face it, 'Everything she do just turns me on' is an uncomfortable line to sing in front of strangers who all feel extreme pity for you.

After putting my name on the list, I sat at the bar with a lemonade looking petrified and waiting for them to call my name, going over the lyrics in my head. An hour later I approached the karaoke host again.

'It was too busy so we had to take your name out,' he said. 'If anyone pulls out we'll put you on.'

So I sat down and waited again. The thing that shocked me was that he said it was too busy and yet every time one of his mates walked through the door he got them straight on, hugging them and patting them on the back while thrusting the mic into their hands, and some of them didn't even want to sing!

I felt a mixture of frustration, anger, relief and boredom. I stuck around until an old boy in a flat cap sang 'Every Little Thing She Does Is Magic' to his dancing wife, everyone clapping along, and then I decided it was time to go. I didn't have a back-up tune and this guy had a reasonable voice, so there was no way I was going to follow him with the same song and butcher it while no one danced or clapped along with me. I could've asked his wife to keep dancing for the James Acaster version but she seemed out of breath after his rendition and anyway it wouldn't have meant the same coming from me. It was eleven p.m. when I left the pub and way too late to find something else to do, so I just went home.

I had immediately failed my own challenge. But despite the fact I had fallen at the first hurdle, I still decided to keep on with it and see how many nights out of seven I could do something new on. Also, maybe going to a bar and attending a karaoke night on your own while crapping yourself because you're expecting to sing a song at any minute also counts as a new experience? I had never even got that far before when it came to singing karaoke. For the first time I had got myself into the right mindset – I was ready to sing in front of a room full of strangers. If I managed to do something different on the other six nights of the week, I could surely allow this as a small victory too. Anyway, it was my challenge so that meant I got to decide the rules.

Board Games

I already knew what I was doing on Thursday night because I had found it when searching 'Things to do on a Wednesday night in Kettering' the previous evening. The Kettering Board Games Club met at the Mind Centre every Thursday. It started at seven p.m. and you had to bring a board game with you – those were the only details the Kettering Board Games Club web page had to offer. So I phoned my friend Wardy (the sign thief) and he agreed to come along as well, because why not?

I brought a board game called Thrice with me. Thrice is a 'simple game of tactics' where you roll three or four die and then leapfrog them over one another as if they were counters on a board, and if you jump over your opponent's dice I believe that means something, maybe you win, I'm not sure. All I knew was I couldn't bring

Monopoly or something obvious like that (this was the Kettering Board Games Club, mainstream games would not be welcome), but I also couldn't bring anything too obscure because then I'd look like I was trying too hard. This 'simple game of tactics' was perfect for the Kettering Board Games Club. It would show that I was smart but not arrogant and that I didn't follow the masses but I also avoided pretension. We knocked on the door of the Mind Centre, Thrice in my backpack, and the door was answered by a bearded man in a *Star Trek* T-shirt (I know that sounds clichéd but it's what happened). He looked at us, perplexed.

'We're here for the board games club!' I said. He looked shocked, literally reacting like no one had ever turned up to Kettering Board Games Club before. Like it had only ever been him, sitting in a room, week after week, hand frozen in a 'flick' position and poised above a spinner, waiting for someone to walk in and challenge him to a game of Articulate.

'Oh, OK, cool, come on up,' he said, having composed himself. We followed him upstairs and into the room where the games took place and it's fair to say I wasn't fully prepared for what awaited me.

I was not, and still am not, familiar with games such as Dungeons & Dragons or Warhammer, but that's what they were playing. There was a game that looked like D&D but was actually called something like Hero Quest being played by two guys on one table, a game that seemed to just involve cards with magic people on them being played by three other fellas on another table (Magic the Gathering?) and a third table where a game that seemed to focus on one of the World Wars was being played by our host and another guy. These games had clearly not been started tonight – they had each been going on for months on end and would continue to last for many months thereafter.

Everyone eyed us up with suspicion and I decided to leave Thrice where it was, firmly in the backpack.

Side note, there was not a single board in sight. No boards. At Kettering Board Games Club. The name of the club was misleading and I don't think this particular misunderstanding had been my fault.

I wasn't sure if they'd let us join in, considering we clearly had no idea how to play the games in question. If they refused to let us play non-board games with them then maybe I could sing 'Every Little Thing She Does Is Magic' for them all and get last night's goal done and dusted instead? After all, at least five of them were huge fans of magic so might have appreciated a song about how great magic is.

But the guy who greeted us at the door was on our side. 'You can play this First World War game over here if you like. One of you can partner me and the other can partner Chris.'

We agreed and I sat next to Chris, who was thirteen or there-abouts and had zero respect for me.

Before the game could begin, the guy who met us at the door asked the question that had to be asked. 'Who wants to be the Germans?'

And I said, 'We will' as soon as he had finished his sentence.

This caused the whole room to look at me as if I were an actual German spy. I was just trying to get the game started quickly but apparently you should never volunteer to be the evil Germans.

Chris rolled his eyes. 'Fine, but I'm not happy about it.' Yeah, shut up, Chris.

The game was hard and really complicated. We had to roll a bunch of dice at the same time (similar to Thrice but with a million dice) but each die meant something different: where we could shoot them, how much damage we'd do, how many bullets we used up, how many steps we could walk, etc. And Chris was not suffering me lightly. Every time I made a decision he'd say, 'Great, you do you realise we're going to lose now?' or, 'Nice one, I hope you like losing,' or, 'Would you like me to roll the dice for you?' It turned out that Chris had actually written the rules to this game himself and we were testing them out for him. And he was now on the losing team, thanks to me. I could kind of see why he was so cross. I was making him lose at his own game, and he'd probably been up late figuring out all the rules and regulations, and then I'd walked in off the street and demolished all of his dreams within seconds. I noticed something familiar about the British soldiers and after asking Chris I learned that yes, he had painted them all to look like the characters from *Dad's Army*. At one point I had to decide whether to shoot Pike in the chest or the face. And I chose the face.

Even though I was awful at the game and Chris invented it, *he* lost all of his soldiers before *I* lost all of mine (up yours, Chris) and so the last moments of the game consisted of me fending off Corporal Jones and Godfrey from behind a rock before Fraser killed me with a long range shot from a tree he'd been hiding in. Chris was full of pure rage and so the other KBGC members sent him to the kitchen to calm down (I got the feeling this was not the first time Chris had blown his stack and been sent to the kitchen to calm down) and when he returned he brought back a packet of plain digestive biscuits even though there were caramel digestives in there, because we 'hadn't earned the nice ones'.

When we got up to go and said goodbye to everyone, none of

the gamers looked up at us or acknowledged our farewells as they were way too engrossed. One of the people on the Hero Quest table didn't hear what we said as he was too busy placing a card on the table in front of his opponent before grinning and saying, 'H-ho! Looks like Greavesy wants a word with your wolflord!' I still don't know what that means but as we descended the stairs towards the exit I heard the other guy say, 'I have been fearing this moment for quite some time.'

Wrestling

I thought it would be easy to find a new thing to do on Friday night, but actually there wasn't a great deal of variety on offer in terms of activities in Kettering. One of the few options available to me was line dancing. Kettering has two line dancing classes a week but absolutely nothing going on on a Friday night. I started to worry but then, fortunately, I struck gold.

I had never been to watch wrestling before. I had never really been a fan when all of my friends were watching it on TV back in my school days and the poster for this event looked like it was very much in the same vein – men looking like cartoon characters pointing and roaring at the camera – but I thought I'd at least be able to make fun of it afterwards when I told friends about it.

If you haven't been to watch live wrestling before you owe it to yourself to go. And if you already go and watch live wrestling, why are you not going more often? Yes it's scripted but so is *The West Wing* and that's why it's amazing. I wish every sport was scripted: there'd be no nil-nil draws and I wouldn't miss a game if the World Cup had a storyline to it. Imagine if players had vendettas against each other and were doing speeches about it beforehand, and not sporting vendettas but personal ones, unforgivable wrongs. Say if Cantona had stolen Le Tissier's car and crashed it into the stadium before the match and now Le Tissier was out for revenge and had announced that if his team won then Cantona had to buy him seven new sports cars or face the consequences and then at half time we learned that Cantona had been having an affair with Le Tissier's wife so they decided to play the match one-on-one, everyone else sitting on the sidelines while they competed for one lady's affections. Gripping, well paced, purely scripted drama. I'd watch it every day. But sadly such things do not exist in football and so I haven't watched a single game since I was thirteen, hence why the only footballers I can name are Eric Cantona and Matt Le Tissier.

I loved wrestling as much as I loved line dancing and I may be the only person who's ever said that (apart from the wrestling world champ Dancing Joe The Dosey Doe Dynamo, who most people haven't heard of because I just made him up).

This particular wrestling event was held in a community centre and the room was packed with a much broader range of people than I had expected. There was of course a big wrestling ring in the middle of the room (much like the boxing ring Pindrop had performed in once upon a time) and the audience were sat around, cheering and clapping and stamping feet. The majority of the evening was a Royal Rumble, which was perfect because you got to see loads of wrestlers coming and going, all doing special moves. Some of my favourites included Shamu (a large gentleman who jumped off the top rope like a killer whale jumping out of the water) and The Spin Doctor (a man dressed as a doctor who would spin around in circles until he hit someone. He lasted five seconds, left the ring, then had to sneak back in because he had forgotten his lab coat). I was caught up in the excitement like nobody's business. I'm usually quite reserved but tonight I was a hardcore wrestling fanatic and screaming the names of my favourites as loud as the next person, which meant I was mainly shouting, 'Go on, Shamu!' for one and a half hours (behaviour that would surely get me kicked out of Sea World).

After the Royal Rumble there was one more fight, a grudge match between good guy, Lion Heart, and all-round baddie, The Judge. They came out and trash-talked for a long time, mainly The Judge being mean and running his mouth off, calling Lion Heart nasty names and being out of order. Then Lion Heart took the mic and held his hand in the air until everyone was silent.

'Before we do this, I want to say a few words about someone very special. She's with us tonight, she's been here at every single show we've ever done, and every time she comes she brings with her an amazing group of youngsters who provide such support and encouragement to every fighter in this ring. We're incredibly grateful to her for the amazing work she does with these kids, so please everyone give a big round of applause to Lynne as she joins us up here in the ring. Come on Lynne, we've got something for you!'

What a lovely speech! Lynne looked genuinely surprised and slowly climbed into the ring, the crowd clapping and cheering, the kids that she worked with going crazy. Lion Heart handed her a beautiful bunch of flowers; even The Judge was applauding her. As the applause died down Lynne said thank you to everyone, Lion Heart gave her a cheeky little kiss on the cheek and she began to return to her seat. But The Judge also had something to say. He took the mic from Lion Heart and put a hand on Lynne's shoulder.

'I would also like to say thank you, Lynne, you do inspiring work with young people in the local area, it means the world and... can I see those flowers quickly, please?' Lynne handed The Judge the flowers and he threw them on the floor and repeatedly stamped on them like a madman. He went ballistic, manically stamping on them until they were in tatters. And guess what? the whole audience turned on him. What few supporters he had were against him now. Bad move you stupid judge wanker, I hope you lose now more than ever! She does amazing work with kids, you scumbag! Let the fight commence!

The Judge

Lynne sat down and the match kicked off. Interesting fact about Lion Heart – every time he gets punched he does a mini roar like a lion cub. And Lion Heart was getting punched A LOT, like it properly looked like The Judge was going to win and if that flower-stomping bully won this fight I didn't know how I was going to react. I'd be inconsolable; I'd be a wreck is what I'd be. The Judge delivered a heavy blow to the face of Lion Heart and he fell to the floor. He was rolling around growling like a little cat as The Judge picked up his gavel and raised it high in the air above him, but the crowd got firmly behind Lion Heart, their cheers making him stronger by the second, and the more we cheered the more energised he became. He started encouraging us to cheer more because that's definitely where he was getting his power from, and I was going bananas. I've never cheered so loudly. My whole face was vibrating. I just didn't want Lion Heart to get it with the gavel. And then Lion Heart used every bit of strength in his entire body... to kick The Judge in the balls. That's how he won. With a shot to the nuts. It was perfect and I've never felt so elated.

The following day I attended a martial arts class. This was the thing I think I enjoyed least all week. The martial art in question was called Jeet Kune Do, a martial art I have never heard of before or since. I was paired with a seventeen-year-old guy who told me he was 'sick of taking shit from people all the time' and then I let him punch me for two hours. I was holding up pads, sure, but he put all of his might into every punch. Every time he hit me I had the urge to roar like Lion Heart but as no one else in the class was doing animal noises I opted not to. At one point he hit me incredibly hard with his left hand and when I said, 'That's quite the left hook,' he paused and nodded, 'Yeah, I'm a south paw,' then punched me in the hand again.

The teacher was an interesting guy because he looked weedy

like Rick Moranis but was a master of three types of martial arts. I talked to the other students and apparently on five separate occasions he has beaten the crap out of men in town on a Friday night because they were sure they could pick on him and didn't anticipate him being a martial arts sensei. Another student told me that the teacher had once chased burglars down the street while waving a samurai sword in the air. Good for him.

And so I had one more day to go. I had done a new thing every night (bar Wednesday, but I've made my feelings clear on that). If I could do something on Sunday night that I'd never done before I would have succeeded. But I didn't. I didn't do something I'd never done before, I did something I'd done many times in the past, and I failed. There was nothing to do on Sunday night! Not even karaoke. Wouldn't that have been great, if I'd gone back to the karaoke pub and done karaoke on the final night? But no, they only did it twice a week. There was nothing, nothing whatsoever, just church stuff, and thanks to my Christian upbringing I had already done plenty of church stuff in my life. You might think, *never mind James, you discovered you love line dancing and going to the wrestling, you got two new pastimes out of just one week.* And you'd be right, only I didn't keep either of them up. I've never done either one of them ever again (apart from wrestling but that was because I took part in a comedy wrestling match at the Edinburgh festival). And even though I had enjoyed two of the activities I didn't much like the board games and the martial arts. Although worst-case scenario would've been the people from the board games club being at the martial arts class. Especially Chris, who probably still hated me for making him lose. He would've obliterated me at martial arts class, probably would've dressed up as a *Dad's Army* character then roundhoused me in the mouth. Yes, things could've gone worse and this little project had certainly passed the time. Five out of seven isn't too bad, is it? Basically, a working week with the weekend off, more or less. So a working week of new things, if not the entire week. Right? No, I can't get out of this. I failed. Well and truly.

Shame

The next story is something I still feel bad about. Whenever I do something I'm not proud of I tend to carry it with me for a long time. For example, the thing I feel most guilty about in my entire life happened when I was twelve years old and involves eating some wild strawberries. My mother, who is the nicest person in the world, had been growing wild strawberries in the garden for months and months. Wild strawberries are much smaller than regular strawberries, not much bigger than a blueberry, and from what I can tell they're not easy to grow. After dinner one day my mum served me and my dad our desserts and then she smiled proudly and said, 'I know what I'm finally having for pudding today!'

'Is it time for the wild strawberries?' asked my dad, and she nodded excitedly. She then disappeared into the garden and returned, cupping a small pile of strawberries in both hands. She washed them and put them into a bowl – she had barely got half a bowlful but the work that had gone into them had been immense. She put a little yoghurt on them and sat down with a spoon. She got a spoonful, leaving only three small strawberries in the bowl.

'Do you want to try them?' she asked my dad. He leaned in and pretended to eat the whole spoonful as a joke and they both laughed, then he took two from the spoon and ate them.

'Would you like to try some, James?' my mum asked me. I had watched my dad's joke and thought it was funny but could've been funnier. I knew what it needed. With humour, you need to push boundaries and go as far as you can go, that's the secret to a great joke, I knew it. I leaned in and just went for the big laugh. As soon as my lips met around the strawberries and I was past the point of no return, I knew I'd messed up. My mouth was clamped over the spoon, all the wild strawberries were in my mouth now. I looked up at my mother who was still holding the handle of the spoon and she looked horrified. I realised what I'd done, I had destroyed something she'd worked hard for, I had taken a simple pleasure in her life and thrown it away. And it still feels like the worst thing I've ever done. The wild strawberries. I don't even remember what they tasted like.

I feel worse about the wild strawberries than I do about the next story, which is weird because many of you will think this next story is much, much worse.

Three Line Whip split up when I was twenty. My friend Graeme and I then formed a new band, a band that would shatter all music that had ever come before it, a new sound for a new age of the human race. The band was called The Wow! Scenario and the band members were me and Graeme. Because there were only two of us we had a slight problem. We desperately wanted to be in a band with sweet, Beach Boys-esque vocal harmonies. Graeme had sung in Three Line Whip but I had still not gotten over my phobia of singing in public thanks to *The Woodcutter and the Christmas Dove* and 'La La La Humpty' and the failed karaoke night.

However, we were tired of recruiting new people to join our bands. I realised that if we were going to drive this band forward in the direction we wanted it to go in, then it was up to me to get over my phobia and learn how to sing from scratch. I knew I wouldn't be able to teach myself so I found a singing teacher who taught from her home in Kettering and she ended up teaching me to sing every week for three years. Oh, and spoiler alert, to this day I still can't sing.

My singing teacher was a lady called Melissa and please don't let my lack of talent reflect badly on her. She did a sterling job, I was just a lost cause. The first lesson I had with her I remember having to sing along to her playing some scales on the piano and she actually turned to me and said, 'I can't teach you.' That was within five minutes of my first lesson. I was determined though and said, 'Give me a load of stuff to practise and if I come back next week and I've not improved at all then we can stop the lessons.' I did two hours' singing practice a day over the next week and returned to Melissa's house having marginally improved, so she agreed to keep teaching me. It took her three years to teach me to sing as well as the average person can sing along to the radio in their car. That was ten years ago though so I'm probably back to square one now as I haven't practised in a long old time.

I got to know Melissa pretty well. Once when she went abroad to visit friends she asked me to house sit for her and I said yes. House sitting was fairly easy; the only responsibility I had was to look after the cat, a rather fussy creature named Mischa. Mischa was a neurotic animal who was always worried she wasn't about to get exactly what she wanted, so never ever stopped mewing. The noise in the house was constant as she walked around relentlessly trying to get her own way. Melissa told me that when I went for a wee I should never lock the bathroom door as Mischa liked to drink from the bidet while you were urinating. Was I supposed to operate the bidet while I went for a wee or did Mischa do that herself with her paws? I was supposed to operate it? Well then no, absolutely not. So every day when I went for a wee in that house I would receive some louder than usual mewing at the door because someone wanted to get in on the bathroom party.

Once the house sitting was over, Melissa told me to keep the keys because she would be needing me to house sit again at some point and so I did as I was told. Some important details you need to know at this stage: Melissa lived near the town centre and I lived just over an hour's walk away from her, and back then I not only had a phobia of singing in public but I also had a phobia of taking a dump in a public toilet. My worst nightmare would've been having a dump in a public toilet while singing 'A Woodcutter's Prayer' to mask the sound of my own bowels. So naturally one afternoon I was in the town centre and all of a sudden I had to go, urgently. I didn't know what to do. There was no way I was using a public toilet and the walk back to my house would take an hour. The only person I knew who lived nearby was Melissa. I rang Melissa's doorbell hoping that she would let me in to use her toilet but no one answered. No one was home. And so I made a split second decision and let myself into somebody else's house, without them knowing, when they weren't there. I know, I know.

I ran straight to the downstairs bathroom, closed the door and immediately did the biggest dump of my life so far. Naturally Mischa came along to investigate, mewing at the damn door, but to be fair I wasn't supposed to be in her house today so she could behave any way she pleased. I finished, breathed a sigh of relief then looked to my left and, nightmare of all nightmares – no toilet paper. If you've ever done a big dump and then turned to the toilet roll holder to find it bare you'll know there is no panic like it. Well, imagine doing that when you're currently intruding in someone else's house. It was terrifying. I was so scared I nearly did a second dump out of pure panic. I had to think fast. There was only one thing I could do. I knew there was a second toilet upstairs, so I could go there and use the toilet paper from the upstairs toilet or use the bidet up there as the downstairs toilet was annoyingly bidet-free. Even if you agree with the first part of this plan you probably won't agree with my next decision.

I chose to leave my shoes, trousers and boxer shorts behind in the downstairs toilet, discarding them because I thought they would only slow me down. I didn't want to pull them back up for obvious reasons, I didn't want them round my ankles and for some insane reason it didn't even occur to me that I could have carried them upstairs with me.

What followed was a real low point in the old life. As I slowly ascended the stairs, naked from the waist down, with a dirty butt, in someone else's house without their knowledge, all I could think was *please don't let anyone come home right now*, because the staircase was directly in front of the front door. If anybody opened that door they would be greeted by my sullied rear end staring down at them from above. I was shaking. To make matters worse, Mischa was following me the entire way mewing her head off. Directly behind me, pretty much mewing at my butt, learning the hard way what a bidet is actually meant to be used for.

Luckily for me I made it to the bathroom without anybody coming home and luckier still there was toilet paper there. I took care of business and felt relieved until I flushed and then it dawned on me why leaving my trousers and pants in the down-stairs toilet wasn't such a smart idea after all. I now had to descend the stairs while cupping myself, once again praying that no one arrived home right at that very moment. It would be bad if Melissa got home now but it would be worse if her husband, who I didn't know well enough, arrived home because he may kill me. Because I was so worried, all I could do was look at the door as I walked down the stairs so if someone did come home I would've been staring at them while covering my modesty, a small black cat making a racket at my ankles and when I explained myself, well, I imagine that would only make matters worse.

I ran into the downstairs bathroom and hurriedly put on my boxers and trousers. I put my shoes on but didn't tie them up as I wanted to get out as soon as possible, I ran out of the bath-room, across the hallway and, just as I was about to leave the house, realised I had forgotten to flush the downstairs toilet. Don't worry – I ran back, flushed and then left – but imagine if I hadn't realised in time. If I had made it all the way home before realising I had not flushed the downstairs toilet, and Melissa's husband had come home to discover an entire poo sitting in his downstairs toilet but no toilet paper in the bowl. Like someone had snuck into his house and done nothing but floaters and then left. I sort of wish that happened because as it stands, I never got my comeuppance for what I did that day. I just got away with it! I deserved to forget to flush and leave evidence behind and then Melissa would have had to deduce that it was someone with a key as there was no sign of a break-in. Maybe they'd send the contents of the toilet to a lab for testing and figure out it was me that way, and I would be stripped of my keys and never be allowed in their house again. But no, I carried on having singing lessons and carried on house sitting, and never told her! Obviously I will have to tell her now that I've written this book and I'm not looking forward to that. In fact I will add another paragraph after this story so you can know how that panned out. In fact, here it is below:

In April 2017 I emailed Melissa a full confession about what happened that fateful day in Kettering. I also sent her the chapter that you have just read in full so that she could approve it for inclusion in these fine memoirs. Her response was not what I expected:

'I did not get what you did with the strawberries. Did you gulp them? Did you throw them away? Did you take hers or the remainders?'

So just to clear everything up – I gulped them. I gulped my mother's spoonful of wild strawberries and left her with just the remainders. I gulped them all. I also let myself into Melissa's house when no one was in and took a secret crap in the toilet, then walked upstairs half naked to clean myself up, then walked back downstairs, still semi nude, got dressed, let myself out and never told her about it. But she had no questions about that whatsoever. Just the wild strawberries. Which we've established I did indeed gulp.

W's

The Wow! Scenario used to practise at a place called the William Knibb Centre in Kettering. My friend Sid worked there and as we were packing away one evening he had some exciting news for us: 'A youth centre in Corby has two yellow polystyrene W's that they're looking to give away for free. They're both about the same size as a bass drum, so you could put one either side and it would say WOW. Do you want them?'

A few days later I drove to the address Sid had given me. I was in my parents' car, can't remember what make it was now but it was small and I hadn't written it off. I know it was small because I was unable to fit the W's inside of it. Mainly, because each W was not 'the size of a bass drum', they were the size of an entire drum kit. They were massive, not just tall but deep and wide as well. All three dimensions were working against me and it was impossible to fit one in my car, let alone two. Sid may have played down the size of these monstrosities, but now I saw how big they were I wanted them even more. They would look so cool on stage and I had to have them. I tried tying the W's to the roof of my parents' car but when I drove away they quickly slipped out of place and fell in front of my windscreen. The caretaker at the youth centre stepped forward and suggested he phone his friend who had a van. So he rang the van man and the van man stopped having dinner with his wife in order to help me. I felt awful about this but it was too late now, the van man was on his way to help someone he'd never met before transport two things that he didn't need back to his house.

I drove home, looking in my rear view mirror at the van man and his wife following me in the van man's van, and kept on feeling guilty. Occasionally I asked myself why I was doing this. Maybe I thought these W's would be the answer, maybe if the band had giant yellow W's on stage we would finally start to build a fan base, maybe we'd get a record deal, we'd headline Glastonbury. Maybe I was still feeling a bit existential since the car crash and now couldn't say no to anything and had to follow everything through, no matter how ludicrous it seemed. Or maybe I just thought it'd be cool to have two giant yellow W's knocking around the house. Whatever the case, I felt like I might have gone too far.

As we pulled into my parents' driveway I remember my dad leaning out of an upstairs window topless, shouting, 'No no no no no' over and over again, waving his arms to try and shoo the W's away from the house. I told the van man to leave before my dad could get downstairs. I would suffer the consequences alone. I offered him some money but he pushed it back into my hand.

'All I ask is that you remember the Van Man,' he said. And as you can see, I have done just that.

My dad didn't deserve this, he was a good man who had supported his son every step of the way, even when he started an experimental jazz/pop band with his friend Graeme, and now I'd started to bring novelty size letters home for no apparent reason.

It took an hour to get both of them into my bedroom and once they were in my room I had virtually no space left in which to move around. There was already a drum kit in my room AND a toy alligator the size of an adult human being. I had won the alligator at a county fair in North Walsham when I was seven. He wore a neon-pink top hat and a T-shirt that said 'Party Gator' across the chest. I named him after Manchester United right-winger Andrei Kanchelskis and my parents hated him because he was enormous and didn't need to exist.

Andrei Kanchelskis

Now that the W's were here, they hated Andrei Kanchelskis even more and maybe even liked their eldest son a little less. I would put forward all of the classic arguments that teens throw at their parents when it comes to their bedrooms: it's my room not yours, you don't ever have to come in here if you don't want to, I'll put up with the lack of space caused by two giant yellow W's and a Party Gator, not you. But every time they caught a glimpse of the inside of my bedroom, their blood would boil.

And considering how upset my parents were at the arrival of the W's you would think I wouldn't, under any circumstances, deliberately acquire more of them, much less go out of my way to do so. But that's precisely what I did. Because I'm a real great son.

The size of a W compared to James Acaster aged 21

About a week later and The Wow! Scenario had a gig in Northampton. We were approached by a photographer who wanted to do a shoot with us wearing our outfits. (Our friend's mum had made these for us. The outfit was a grey T-shirt with a black shirt collar sewn on to it, black school trousers, navy blue slip-ons and a homemade yellow tie that stuck on to the front of the T-shirt with velcro. We called them WowFits. Shut up.) We were well up for this photoshoot, especially because we now had these yellow W's in our possession (they were still in my bedroom as we were unable to transport them to gigs – my parents were understandably furious when they learnt we hadn't found any practical use for them). But when we told the photographer about these W's he shrugged and said, 'Oh no need to bother, I've already got one.'

And then he showed us a photo on his phone of exactly the same sort of giant yellow W as the ones I had in my room. He told us he had been given the W by a company called Connexions. He explained that Connexions was an organisation that helped young people decide what they wanted to do with their lives, after school, college or university. They provided information on the steps you could take in order to achieve your goals. They had recently launched a campaign in Northamptonshire entitled 'What Next?', and as part of this campaign, a giant yellow W (W for What Next?) was delivered to every branch of Connexions across the county and, according to our photographer friend, the staff at Connexions hated the W's even more than my parents did.

'They're desperate for people to take them off their hands so I said I'd have one in case I needed it for photos. That's probably where your W's came from too,' the photographer said (the next day I checked with the youth centre who gave us the W's and they confirmed they were indeed from Connexions).

My friend Emma was at the gig and later that night I told her about the big coincidence with this man having the same W as the ones we had. I explained the whole backstory regarding the Connexions people and how much they hated the W's and Emma had a suggestion to make: 'If they don't want them we should go round taking them off their hands until we've got every single one and then you can do a gig where you fill the stage with yellow W's.' Not only did I agree to this plan but I was so on-board that we sorted out the day we'd start the project – Saturday – there and then. Full disclosure: we were both really into Dave Gorman at the time (still am) and maybe his adventures had rubbed off on us. When you're in your early twenties and feel a bit aimless, hearing stories about a man finding meaning in the apparently meaningless is extremely inspiring. Maybe this was our Dave Gorman moment? Maybe we would meet a whole host of characters through gathering these W's and in doing so understand more about ourselves and our fellow man? This could bring people together! I went home and looked forward to Saturday.

The day rolled around and, against all logic, neither of us had backed out. And so we drove to Wellingborough in Emma's car (which was as small as my parents' car) to pick up an item that we knew would not fit inside our vehicle. I began to wish I'd kept the van man's number but then again he might not have appreciated me making this his full-time job: picking up W's, dropping them off at my parents' house, then speeding away before my dad could catch him, shouting 'Remember the Van Man' out of his van window as he screeched round the corner. No, we had to figure this one out by ourselves – we were Dave Gorman now.

The Wellingborough branch of Connexions had the W in the

window with a bunch of flyers strewn across it. We walked in and sat in the waiting area. As we waited, I started to feel bad because everyone in the queue before us was waiting to ask for help figuring out their own way forward in life and we were about to ask for something utterly pointless. I also began to doubt they'd really give it to us. Their W was in the window on display and they seemed to be using it. What if it was just the Northampton branch that hated their W and the Wellingborough branch was actually rather fond of theirs and we were about to come across as rude and weird and then we'd have to leave while everyone gave us funny looks all the way out the door? Maybe this is exactly the sort of behaviour that warrants an intervention from the people at Connexions. I didn't think I needed help figuring out what I wanted to do with my life but once I told them what I'd come there for they might beg to differ.

'Can I help you?' said a kind-faced lady.

Emma answered with confidence. 'Can we have that W in the window?'

The kind-faced lady breathed a sigh of relief. 'Please just take it, we hate it so much, thank you!' She didn't even ask why we wanted it. One of the younger women who worked there wanted her photo taken with the W before we left because she'd always wanted to sit on top of it. We got a photo of her sitting atop the W giving the double thumbs up, looking as though she'd just achieved a lifelong dream. This was exactly the sort of stuff we were hoping for! Bringing people together, making people's days, using the absurd to break down the walls that separate us all! We were so Dave Gorman.

We had parked further away than was ideal. The car was about a twenty minute walk away, the W was huge and bright yellow, and we were attracting a lot of attention. Some kids on bikes began to follow us, shouting stuff like 'W is for wanker!' at me. Normally when kids are shouting this kind of stuff at me I would either ignore them, reply in a sensible manner, or make the mistake of trying to sass them back. In this instance I was in such a good mood post-getting-a-W that I found their jibes hilarious and sort of just agreed with them, which weirdly endeared me to them. Before long these three teenagers were pretty much our friends and thought that me and Emma carrying a giant yellow W around Wellingborough was awesome (W is for cool more like!!!).

When we reached the car the teenagers got worried. 'How you gonna fit it in there, mate?' But Emma had come prepared. She opened the boot and pulled out a saw.

'Two V's,' she stated. Soon I was lost in a cloud of polystyrene snow as I sawed the W in half. We had turned it upside down (it was now an M, strictly speaking) and Emma and one of the teenagers were holding it steady for me. One half went in the boot, the other in the back of the car and we received legit high fives from our new friends before they cycled away shouting 'W! W! W!' over and over again like an aggressive website address (Dave. Gorman.) It had begun; we couldn't stop now. Emma decided she would keep the V's in her garage and looked up where all the Connexions were in Northamptonshire so we could continue our mission the following weekend. Then I received a text from my photographer friend: 'Would you like this W? I've no use for it.'

Some friends of ours were walking past the Northampton branch of Connexions on their way back from the pub one night and spotted a giant yellow W next to a nearby skip. They carried it all the way home and put it in their living room. We were grateful but confused because we thought the photographer's W had come from Northampton but it turned out it had not and if we wanted to collect *his* W then we would have to go to the town of Isham and we would have to do it this week or his boss was going to make him throw it away. Emma was far too busy that week and I had no use of the car so I texted my friend Matt and asked for help, because he had a big car with a roof rack and I didn't want to saw all of the W's in half (one was fine but not all of them; it felt like a cop-out).

Matt was married with a child so I thought he would say no, but it turns out that if you're married with a child this sort of distraction is even more enticing.

We turned up at the photographer's studio and were surprised when we saw the W he had waiting for us. In the photo he'd shown me back in the bar the W looked exactly the same as our W's, but this one was different. This W was still encased inside a giant white rectangle of polystyrene – it hadn't been popped out yet. Turns out he'd shown us a photo of a different W because he didn't have a photo of this one, which, considering he was a photographer, seemed a little bit odd to me but then again you can't expect someone to have a photograph of everything they've ever seen simply because they are a photographer.

We tied it to the roof rack and proceeded home at a conservative pace. (Imagine the risks if we hadn't. Imagine a giant yellow W becoming airborne on the motorway, spinning through the air. It'd be worse than knocking out a cow with a slip-on. Oh and don't worry, this isn't the story of my second car crash, although I'm fully aware this story feels like it's heading that way.) My parents had made it very clear to me that there were to be no more W's in their house (a rule I'm sure no one else has ever had imposed upon them ever) and so Matt agreed to keep it in his house until I found a better place for it. We put it in his bedroom and it took up an entire wall. We did this while his wife was not home. When she returned home she was far from impressed.

Kettering Connexions was easy to hit up. Emma just popped in one day and walked away with another two W's that we stashed in her sister's garage.

Over the next few weeks I would receive a text message from Matt every other day asking me when I could collect the W, each time emphasizing the toll the W was taking on his marriage. The problem I had was that Emma had got a new job. When we started the quest, she was unemployed and looking for a project to pass the time and the W's had kept her nice and busy for a while. But then she'd found employment sooner than expected and so had to stop driving around the county collecting W's for no reason. Things weren't looking good. In fact, things were looking as bad as they could be. If we'd completed the challenge we'd have felt great, if we'd never have started it we would've felt relieved, if we'd been able to use the W's for anything useful at all we would have been proud of ourselves and would've looked like winners when everyone else had doubted us. But instead we now had seven giant yellow W's stored in five different houses and had absolutely no use for any of them whatsoever. You usually only hear about crazy challenges like this when they're a success. When they're a success they're strangely life-affirming and uplifting like the

Dave Gorman books we'd both read, but when they are a failure they just remind you that life is stupid and unfair and we as human beings are the biggest idiots of all. If Dave Gorman had met five or six other people named Dave Gorman and then had to pack it in because no one else wanted to meet up with him then he'd have looked very silly but instead he achieved his goal, he won the bet with his friend and has come out the other end a bona fide legend. I hadn't been able to do a new thing every day for a week and now I had failed to collect a bunch of giant yellow W's. I was a laughable individual, needlessly attempting challenges that served little to no purpose and failing them every time.

We threw them all in the tip. One at a time, driving to and from the different locations and the tip itself, we threw them all away. The employees at the tip watched us in amazement, trying to figure out what events could have possibly led to this. We threw all of them away apart from two, the two that I originally collected from the youth centre in Corby. My friend Ben had kindly offered to keep them in his garage. We locked the garage doors and forgot about them for five years and then while sitting in Ben's living room one day we remembered; we remembered that I had acquired these two giant yellow W's and that he had agreed to store them inside his garage. Only he had moved out of that house two years ago and was now living somewhere new. He had not taken the W's with him. That means that there was once a day in history when someone opened the doors of their new garage to discover two giant yellow polystyrene W's staring back at them, completely out of context. They would've had absolutely no way of figuring out why they were there and then they would've had to figure out what to do with them. Knowing that that happened makes the whole thing a little bit worth it. But still, every time I look at my book shelf and see my copy of *Are You Dave Gorman?* I think *No. No I'm not.*

Déjà Vu

After three valiant years, The Wow! Scenario decided to call it quits. Graeme wanted to go travelling and I didn't know what I wanted to do but I couldn't carry on as a solo artist because I was a drummer and my singing was terrible.

The band had one final gig in the diary and it was on a farm in North Yorkshire. I can't remember what the festival was called now but it was being run by a Leeds promoter, a friend of ours called Adam, and was the kind of gig that if we hadn't been splitting up immediately after we would've been really excited about. Independent festivals are usually a huge amount of fun, because they're small but busy and everyone is enthusiastic, so they feel like your own secret gig, and being one of the bands on the bill makes you feel like an integral part of some new and exciting thing that only cool people know about. Our friend George came with us (you remember George, he lived on the other side of my secondary school) because he wanted to film our final show. It took us ages to find the place because it really was a farm in the middle of nowhere, nothing but fields and hillside for miles, but we finally saw a stumpy old boy in high-vis directing traffic towards the site.

We played to about twenty people in the smaller of two tents. There were a lot more people at the festival by then but we were one of the first bands on so everyone was too busy drinking else-where. Every now and then as a performer you have a gig that means more to you than it does to the audience. We didn't mention this was our final gig during our set because that would've felt a little tragic, what with most people not watching us and all. It's fine to announce it's your final gig to a packed room of fans but not to twenty people mooching around who don't know who you are and don't care if you're splitting up because it doesn't make a jot of difference to their lives. We finished the gig and moved our equipment into a wigwam assigned to the acts, then we watched the other bands for a while whilst eating jacket potatoes. I remember being freezing because I only had my WowFit on and so I put my arms inside my T-shirt; then the lead singer of a different band made fun of me from the stage, and the audience turned and laughed. No one had any idea I had been on earlier or that I was even in a band. That sounds sad but at the time it made me feel better as I was officially a punter again.

We had a four-hour drive ahead of us so we left at half past ten in the evening and by two a.m. I was asleep and if you're good at maths you'll know that that's not good. This is the story of the second car crash.

I woke up when Graeme shouted 'Oi!' at the top of his voice

because he'd turned and seen me driving with my eyes closed (obviously he should've taken a leaf out of the skydiver's book and shouted 'We've got a sleeper!' but 'oi!' did the job nicely all the same). I awoke with a jolt and immediately steered to my right and the car sped towards the central reservation of the dual carriageway, so I steered left and we headed straight towards the only other vehicle on the road, a huge lorry, then right again, headed towards the central reservation, then left again and headed towards the lorry. I steered away from the lorry once more and it was at this point that my car decided, 'You clearly can't make up your mind which way you should be going right now, we haven't got all day, so allow me to make this decision for you.' The car started lurching from left to right, up and down and side to side – nothing I was frantically pressing or stamping on was making a difference. Then the car made its choice, speeding towards the central reservation which we hit head on, hard. We then span away and hit the lorry with the back of our car (always nice to end up hitting both of the things you were trying to avoid hitting), then span away and hit the central reservation, then span away and hit the lorry, and we kept doing this over and over, spinning and hitting while still moving forwards down the dual carriageway. I remember all of the windows exploding and showering us with tiny balls of glass. George woke up halfway through, asked what was going on and I said, 'We're crashing.' (I was the only one who had been in a car crash before so I was the most qualified to assess whether or not this was indeed a crash.) And then we stopped. The speed with which Graeme exited the car was remarkable. The second the car stopped moving he opened the door and ran away. George and I took a little longer because we were still taking it in, I think. I remember Graeme shouting from the side of the road, 'Come on!' and me replying, 'No.'

No! What a bold move from someone who has just massively ballsed up, now refusing to actually do something sensible despite the fact he's lucky to be alive. It finally occurred to me that I was sitting in the middle of the dual carriageway, stationary in a broken car with bits of said car strewn across the road behind me, and once I had taken that information on board I too ran out of the car and joined Graeme by the side of the road. George was still sitting in the back so we both shouted to him to 'Get out now' with maximum urgency. He opened the door, walked calmly towards us, then remembered he had left his camcorder inside so walked back to the car, rooted around until he found it, then completed his journey to the grass verge and started filming the wreckage from the roadside, occasionally walking back into the road to get some artier shots. The car itself had seen better days: the front and back weren't there any more, the windows were gone and the one door none of us were sitting next to was completely caved in. The lorry driver ran up to us and checked we were ok, having worried that we'd gone under the lorry. I was certain he was about to give us a ruddy good dressing down but he was just concerned and relieved. We realised that the other side of the dual carriageway was closed and empty so we ran across and stood over there instead. It seemed safer than standing on the grass at least.

The police never showed up, even though we called them, but the recovery service people did and they had a lot to say.

'You know that lorry you hit?' said a man with a torch.

'Yes,' I said, because of course I knew the lorry I hit, I knew it all too well, I knew it intimately thanks.

'It were full of milk!' he squawked; then he gave me a few seconds to allow the information to sink in before adding, 'so if that had fallen on you, you'd have been dead!' I sometimes wonder if this man got home that night and as he was getting into bed realised that the comment he had made about the milk not only made no sense but probably didn't do much to reassure the survivors either. Did he think that if the lorry had not contained milk it would've simply bounced right off us and all would've been well? Or had he sized us up and had us pegged for a bunch of lactose intolerants and so the worst type of lorry to fall on us ever would be a milk lorry because if the impact doesn't kill you, the contents will. Looking back now, I assume the lorry was carrying crates of milk but at the time I just imagined one huge tank of milk on its back, like a gasoline truck, and if it had fallen on us then a tidal wave of semi-skimmed would've been unleashed on the dual carriageway, the townspeople rushing to the side of the road to dunk their biscuits in the milky river as Graeme, George and I melted like the Wicked Witch of the West, the deadly milk taking its toll immediately – we never stood a chance.

As the man with the torch was talking to us, one of the other recovery service people drove past us slowly and yelled, in a voice not unlike Otto from *The Simpsons*, 'HEY BOYS! How does it feeeeeeel? How does it feeeeeel TO BE ALIIIIIIIIIIIIIIIIIVE!!!!' and then sped away. These recovery service guys were a little off.

'Now I've got to ask you, have you been doing any drugs?' the torch guy said (I was about to ask him and his pals the same question.)

'No, never,' I replied. I probably didn't need to say 'never'; saying 'never' was such a suck-up thing to do. 'I've never ever taken drugs and would never dream of it; the only thing I've ever been high on is life. Hugs not drugs – I don't need drugs to have a good time, sir.'

This guy had probably (definitely) done drugs himself and now thought I was king of the squares for never having done so. It was at that moment, right after I had told this man that I'd never done drugs, that George walked over to us, smoking a roll up cigarette, and asked the recovery service guy if he wanted 'a toke on this'. His timing and wording were both incredible. There's no way he could've known what the guy had just asked me and yet as soon as drugs were mentioned that's when he popped up and chose to use terminology only ever associated with smoking cannabis. No one has a toke on a normal cigarette, do they?[4] The recovery service guy seemed to agree with me: he suddenly looked suspicious, sniffed the air a bit, looked at us both, then smiled and said, 'No I'm all right, mate.' Meanwhile I was having a heart attack.

We'd lost a bongo. Some of the recovery service guys were searching for it in the trees by the side of the road. Graeme had lost a guitar too. It was nowhere to be seen and we could only conclude it must've flown out of the car as we were spinning and landed outside the dual carriageway. But mainly, we lost a bongo. Months later George put all the footage from his camcorder on to his computer and while we were watching it back we spotted the lost bongo propped up against the central reservation. How perplexing it must've been for motorists to see a bongo in the middle of the dual carriageway, all of them trying to work out how it had got there. I like to imagine a beat poet crossing the road and abandoning the bongo halfway because it was slowing him down.

Back on the night of the crash the guy with the torch was still inspecting the car and making polite chit-chat. 'So you're in a band are you? When's your next gig?' he asked.

'Never. We just split up,' Graeme said.

---

4 Maybe they do; I've never smoked them either – I'm a very good boy.

The man raised his eyebrows and looked around at the crash site. He nodded, looking somewhat spaced out, taking in what Graeme had said. 'Yeah, man. I suppose you have, haven't you?'

Didgeridoo

After the band split up, I still kept in contact with my singing teacher Melissa because she was cool and because I felt guilty about taking a secret dump in her house. One day she asked me if I would like to come to her house for a jam session. I was still approaching jam sessions with caution since 9/11 (if you've skipped ahead to this chapter then that sentence will seem a lot more intense than intended) but Melissa made this particular jam session sound rather intriguing.

She had a student who she was teaching music theory to; he was in his late forties and could play the didgeridoo. She was grade eight flute and they had been meeting up and jamming together but they felt like they were missing some percussion. They suggested that I play the congas, which was a relief because

I owned a pair of congas – if they'd asked me to play the bongo I'd have been no good to them (unless I fancied risking my life retrieving it from the middle of the A14). And so I said yes. As always I probably need to justify to some of you why I agreed to this. It was simply too unusual to pass up. As far as I was concerned the worst that could happen was we would have a rubbish jam session (although I was more than prepared for 'All Along the Watchtower' should they spring a didgeridoo version on me) and the best that could happen was that I would enjoy playing a different kind of music with other people again. Plus I still didn't know what I wanted to do with my life since the band had split up and was currently open to anything. Maybe this band would be the one, who knows?

I lived quite a long way from Melissa (as you already know) but apparently the didgeridoo player lived in the village across from me so Melissa arranged for him to pick me up after I'd finished work that day and drive me to the jam.

He arrived an hour early. I was still greasy after a day in the kitchen and my body ached after taking several baked potatoes to the nuts (it had been yet another delightful shift for yours truly) and I needed a hot shower. I invited him inside so he could wait in the living room but he refused and sat alone in his car on my driveway. I didn't have time to query his motives. I had a shower, loaded my congas into the back of his car and off we went. Before he'd even got to the end of my street he asked me, 'Do you like conspiracy theories?' There was a pause.

'I don't really believe any of them,' I replied.

'I love them,' he said, then went on to tell me how 9/11 was an inside job (Too right! Those musicians knew I didn't have Hendrix in my repertoire! They set me up!) and revealed that

Gordon Brown had been kidnapping kids in vans and injecting them with diseases.

'Seriously, if you don't believe me, I could show you videos on YouTube.' Great. He continued, 'Melissa said you're a comedian.'

'Well, not really, I did a couple of gigs once.'

'I've written a sitcom. Grant Mitchell is a lorry driver and he tries to fight people at karate but keeps putting people in headlocks all the time.'

I'll never forget his sitcom pitch and I can laugh at his idea all I want but I still remember it all these years later so maybe it's brilliant. Grant Mitchell, not Ross Kemp which is the actor's name, but Grant Mitchell the character from *EastEnders* (enemy of Eco Man) is a lorry driver (which was the didgeridoo player's day job, by the way) and he tries to fight people at karate (why?) but keeps putting people in headlocks all the time. (All the time! I love the thought of every episode involving a scene where he puts someone in a headlock when he was meant to be using a wider range of karate moves on them.) If he was going to make this sitcom he would need a martial arts expert on set. I did consider giving him the address of the Jeet Kune Do class I'd gone to that one time but was worried that the sensei wouldn't take kindly to a conspiracy theorist turning up and ranting about Grant Mitchell, and I didn't want this didgeridoo-ist to end up on the business end of a samurai sword.

We arrived at Melissa's and set up our equipment. There wasn't much pre-jam chat, which was odd, but to be honest I was just glad all the conspiracy theories had stopped and he wasn't pitching sitcoms at me. Mischa walked past the door and gave me a look, a look that said, 'I know what you did,' and I was reminded of how I'd dashed through these very corridors, naked from the waist down, urgently searching for toilet paper after having effectively broken into the premises illegally.

'Thank you so much for doing this, James,' said Melissa, and I looked at the floor in shame, shrugging my shoulders, trying to convey that it was no hassle whatsoever while also trying to stop myself from saying, 'Sometimes I come in here when you're away and go for poos.'

We were ready to play so our didgeridoo-er began the first jam with a long drone on the didgeridoo. I haven't heard a lot of didgeridoo players but I know it isn't easy to do circular breathing so I'm going to say he was actually very good at playing the didgeridoo. It sounded pretty good to me anyhow. Melissa joined in on the flute playing some classical-sounding melody and then I joined in on the congas like an absolute hero.

The first song we jammed lasted about fifteen minutes. It was very experimental and to this day I'd say I haven't heard anything exactly like it, mainly because flute/congas/didgeridoo is not the full line-up of a single band ever. We finished the song (all at the same time too) and looked at each other. There was excitement in Melissa's eyes. I could tell she was happy. I was feeling pretty happy too, considering the journey I'd just had with this man, and I was quite surprised to find myself already considering making this a regular thing from now on because I genuinely enjoyed how the three of us sounded together.

Then the didgeridoo-ist looked at me, furrowing his brow. 'You need to slow down on them congas,' he said. 'You're playing too fast.'

'OK, sure, no problem,' I said before Melissa raised her hand.

'Oh, I don't think we need to tell each other what to do, just keep doing whatever you want to, James, it's fine. Let's play again!'

The second jam lasted roughly twenty minutes and in my opinion sounded better than the first. I did try and play slower, like he asked, and to his credit that had instantly improved the quality of the overall sound of the band. I started trying to think of band names. Maybe All The Kings Men? Rumpty Pumpty? Sunny Side Up? PinYak? So many options.

As the jam came to an end (all together again!) he pointed at me. 'Too slow that time,' he said. 'Speed up the congas a bit.'

'Honestly, James,' Melissa countered, 'just do whatever you like, I think it sounds nice.' He threw Melissa a glare and opened his mouth to speak, but then the doorbell rang. Time had gotten away from us and Melissa's next student had arrived for her singing lesson. She was a sweet woman in her seventies and smiled at us all as she walked into the practice room.

'Oh my! Are you in a band these days, Melissa?' Melissa nodded and then proceeded to tell her how wonderful she thought it was all sounding, how original and unique.

'It's like nothing you've ever heard before, and I'm blessed with two amazing musicians. This one believes the Royal Family are all Lizard People and this one runs around my house covered in shit!' She didn't say those exact words but I read between the lines. The student was completely drawn in by Melissa's enthusiasm.

'Wow, well my son is a record producer, did you know that?' We didn't. 'If you like I can ring him now!' And then she rang him. 'Hello darling, I'm sitting here with a hot new band who'd like to play a song for you, listen!' And then she held the phone out and nodded at us to start playing.

I was stunned. This is the kind of story you'd usually read about in the autobiography of a rock legend, their big break, where everything just falls into place at once and they manage to get a record deal during their first ever practice because they were that awesome. Where was this kind of luck when The Wow! Scenario were still going?!

The man started playing the didgeridoo, Melissa started playing the flute and I joined in with the congas.

The third jam lasted one minute, a good fourteen to nineteen minutes shorter than usual. The man stopped playing the didgeridoo and when we realised he wasn't going to join back in we stopped too.

'Slow down on the congas, you're too fast,' he said, pointing at me without looking at me.

'James, you can really just do whatever you feel like doing,' Melissa said dismissively.

The didgeridoo-ion stood up, his body rigid. He lifted the didgeridoo above his head with both hands and threw it down on the ground (if you've ever been present when a didgeridoo bounces on the ground you'll know it makes quite the satisfying 'doink' sound). Then he fixed both eyes on Melissa, took a deep breath and let it all out.

'I ALWAYS KNEW YOU WERE AGAINST ME FROM THE VERY START OF THIS YOU'VE BEEN PLOTTING BEHIND MY BACK AND TURNING THIS BAND AGAINST ME I WILL NOT LET YOU TAKE THIS AWAY FROM ME YOU CAN'T HAVE CONTROL JUST BECAUSE YOU ARE FROM ITALY AND STUDIED AT SOME FANCY SCHOOL OF MUSIC I ALWAYS KNEW YOU WERE GOING TO ORGANISE A MUTINY YOU THINK I DIDN'T SEE IT

COMING I SAW IT COMING A MILE OFF AND I TOLD MYSELF I WOULDN'T STAND FOR IT AND I'M NOT STANDING FOR IT NOW SO YOU CAN FUCK OFF I WANT NOTHING MORE TO DO WITH YOU EVER DO YOU UNDERSTAND I NEVER WANT TO SEE YOU EVER AGAIN FUCK YOU!!!!!!'

There was a pause, then a tiny voice said, 'Mum?' We all looked at the lady's phone. 'Mum, are you there?'

She left to talk to her son outside while my angry bandmate packed up his didge in fury. He stopped in his tracks just before he walked out the door and looked at me. 'Do you want a lift home?'

'No,' I said, 'I've got to go and meet some friends nearby.'

Later on when I told Melissa that this had been a lie she called me a genius and said that thinking of that lie on the spot had been very, very clever. Having Melissa praise my lies made me feel better about not being completely open with her, and made me consider the possibility that telling her the truth about the most shameful day of my life might not be completely necessary. Although if I was ever going to bring it up I probably should've done it there and then. As soon as that guy told her to fuck off and stormed out of her house I should've casually said, 'Oh by the way, once I let myself in when you were out, had a poo in your downstairs loo but wiped my butt in the upstairs loo and walked round the house in a state of undress between the two.' She wouldn't have loved it but it would've been less of a big deal when coupled with the conspiracy theorist's aggressive outburst and the demise of the band. Maybe he was right – maybe my timing was off. I only wish he was the scariest bandmate I'd teamed up with that year.

Festival

The didgeridoo/flute/conga jam band (clearly we should've been called DidgeriFlute) turned out to be the first of two brief musical ventures after the demise of The Wow! Scenario. The second occurred at a festival.

One of the best festivals in all of Britain, in my opinion, is/ was the Greenbelt Festival. I haven't been for the whole weekend for a long time so can't vouch for what it's like these days but I used to go every year. It was at Cheltenham Race Course and classes itself as a Christian festival. I was raised Christian and continued to be so throughout my teens but I am now agnostic. Greenbelt is pretty much the reason I could never be an atheist *or* a Christian. It was a wonderful place, great atmosphere, full of kind people sharing ideas and having discussions and disagreeing with each other in a respectful manner. I'm sure it didn't mean to teach me this but it taught me that I can never be certain about anything, that leadership in churches is often pretty dodgy, and that there probably is more to life but I will never truly understand it or fully know what it is. Although reading that back I'm not sure if I learnt that at Greenbelt or if that's the kind of philosophy you adopt after numerous scrapes have befallen you. Once you've scoured the county for W's and attended Kettering Board Games Club you accept that you will never be able to fully comprehend the universe.

Greenbelt used to have a chai tea tent every year where people would drink chai tea (not me because it's gross) and every now and then they'd hold a djembe[5] workshop out the front of the tent where everyone sat down in a circle and all played djembes for ages while an old white guy with dreadlocks conducted them. This is why I can never justifiably make fun of hippies or new age types, because I have joined in with that djembe workshop and I totally get why people love it. The djembe jams (let's call them what they are, dJAMbes) would go on for hours and were never interrupted by a didgeridoo player telling you to speed up or slow down – you just did as you pleased. Maybe I should've formed a twenty-piece djembe jam band called dJam and released albums that sound identical but by their very nature cannot be replicated. I could've worn a multi-coloured woven hoodie and grown a little chin beard and changed my name to Leaf and been a vegan. But I didn't do any of those things and now I'm writing a book about how much of a joke my entire life has been.

One year the chai tea tent was also host to some open mic. You

---

5 An African drum that looks like an hourglass-shaped conga.

could put your name on the chalkboard next to an allocated time and then you could stand in the corner of the tent and play whatever you felt like. I was standing next to the chalkboard one morning, watching the djembe players, when a lady, roughly in her forties, with short hair and wearing a big red leather jacket that was maybe two sizes too large, approached the board and let out a sigh.

'Hmmm I want to do open mic but I need a percussionist,' she said to no one, but kind of to me and my friend Matt who had also been drawn in by the djembe players (this is the same Matt who had once harboured a W for me in the bedroom he shared with his wife). It was quite odd hearing her despair about a lack of percussion when the djembe djam was in full flow in front of us; it was a kick in the teeth for the djembe djammers, openly letting them know that she didn't consider a single one of them to be adequate percussionists even by the standards of the chai tea open mic. You'd think Matt, who had now turned to speak to her, would suggest she ask a djembe player to accompany her since they were so readily available, but instead he said, 'James is a drummer, he can do it.' She looked at me, waiting for my answer. I wracked my brains. There was nothing in particular I had planned to do that day, so I said yes because who knows, maybe *this* will be the band I had finally been waiting for, not The Wow! Scenario, not DidgeriFlute; maybe she was the next Joni Mitchell and I was just in the right place at the right time. She put her name on the board next to 16:00, which gave me five hours to find a percussion instrument that wasn't a djembe. (Djembes were for the djembe workshops only: they had a strict no borrowing policy and that included chai tea open mic, despite the fact they were both run out of the same tent by the same people.)

I can't remember where I got it from but I managed to borrow an egg shaker from someone. That is, a shaker in the shape of an egg, not a contraption that shakes eggs. That was all I could find at a Christian festival! You would think there'd be tambourines falling out of everyone's pockets at a Chrizza Fest but how times have changed.

I made it to the chai tea tent at 15:50, worried that I had not brought enough percussion with me. I didn't want to let this lady down, after all it was her name on the board and not mine, and it was her reputation on the line if we choked up there and sounded like garbage. But then she arrived.

From a distance it was difficult to make out what she had brought along with her. I realised I had never asked what instrument she played so had no idea what I'd be accompanying. I had assumed she was a guitarist earlier but she appeared to be carrying a big red bean bag in her arms. It couldn't be a drum because she said she needed a percussionist. As she got closer I could see that she wasn't carrying one big thing but lots of smaller things and they were all wobbling and shaking in her arms as she struggled not to drop them. As she approached the tent all become clear. She was carrying about twenty coat hangers in her arms. A huge pile of red metal coat hangers. It was at this point that I started to worry. I half expected her to start pitching me a sitcom: Miss Marple is a deep sea diver and finds buried treasure but keeps on slapping mermaids, for example.

She entered the chai tea tent and didn't even smile or say hello to me. She just said, 'Come on then,' and I followed her to the part of the tent reserved for the open mic performers. She moved a small wooden coffee table into our performance space, looked at me and said, 'Do you want to start?' Start what?? I thought we were going to be playing some songs she had written; I didn't think this was another frigging jam band. I'd had enough of jamming!!! All I wanted to do was play a song that had been planned out in advance that preferably wasn't a much loved classic I was unfamiliar with. 'I like to jam,' she said, confirming my greatest fears. 'You start.'

So I started to shake the shaker. Just a standard 4/4 rhythm, accentuating the first beat of each bar, classic stuff, playing it safe. She didn't join in for a while; she just watched me. She was the only one watching me too because no one else could even hear me – they were just drinking chai tea and chatting, no idea that a gig had even started. And then she lifted all twenty of the coat hangers above her head, took aim and threw them at the table. It was so similar to how the didgeridoo player had thrown his didgeridoo on the floor that I thought she was quitting the band immediately and was about to launch into a rant about how I was trying to turn the whole band against her. But no, this was apparently how you play the coat hangers. The moment the coat hangers clattered against the wooden table was when everyone turned to look at us. Coat hangers were scattered all over the shop now. She got down on all fours and gathered all of the coat hangers on to the table and started moving them around on the surface while making moaning noises. I maintained the 4/4 rhythm of the egg shaker. Every now and then she would throw another coat hanger at the table or make a high pitched noise like a kestrel swooping in for the kill. After ten minutes (!) of this, she introduced some lyrics to the song. The lyrics were simple and she would shout them every now and again whenever she felt like it. The lyrics in question were 'Reflective surfaces!' and 'Conjoined twins!'. 'Conjoined twins' was always delivered in a much more menacing manner than 'Reflective surfaces', although I feel like if our song had a name it would've been 'Reflective Surfaces'; it just suited the music better I think, plus 'Conjoined Twins' would've been a pretty full-on title for a debut single. Maybe 'Conjoined Twins' was the band name, there were two of us after all, although we had never even hung out together before this performance so calling us conjoined was a bit of a stretch.

She then started doing that thing that horses do with their lips, when they vibrate them and make that horse noise (maybe she did this as an homage to the horses of Cheltenham Race Course, I'll never know) but she did it constantly, spitting everywhere, mainly all over me, mainly all over my face. At one point she picked up a coat hanger and smacked it against the table over and over like a hammer. I thought back to the days of Pindrop and suddenly Lloyd didn't seem that bad. Compared to this he was a consummate professional. And then she closed her eyes and made a low humming noise that only I could hear and stood there swaying on the spot. At this point I did think to myself, *WHY DID SHE NEED A PERCUSSIONIST?!!??* Honestly, what part of this performance would've suffered without the egg shaker???

I was still keeping a steady beat with the shaker, watching her as her hum got gradually quieter and her sways got smaller and smaller, until she was standing still, eyes closed, in silence. The jam ended when I dropped the egg shaker. I had carried on shaking the egg for a while when she had her eyes closed but then decided I would quite like to stop the jam now, so I just let go of the egg and as soon as it hit the floor her eyes opened as if woken from a trance. She blinked, scooped up the coat hangers and left without saying goodbye. One person was applauding us, my friend Matt, tears of joy streaming down his face. At that point he was probably certain that God existed whereas I had most likely lost my faith for ever – vintage Greenbelt.

Walking back to my tent I noticed something that looked a little out of place. There was a short tree, about six feet tall, completely bare, with a dozen branches of varying lengths. The tree looked as though it had been sanded down. It was very smooth and had been sectioned off with tape, as if it was the scene of a crime, and there was a notice on a post next to the tree. At the top of the notice there was a picture of the tree, only it looked different in the picture. In the picture the branches weren't as bare as they were now; in the picture the branches had about twenty red coat hangers hanging from them and under the picture was a paragraph about the tree which, it turns out, was one of many works of art created especially for the festival.

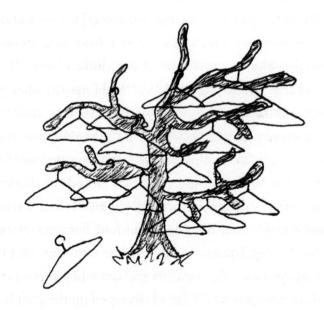

Modern art

She had stolen them. She had stolen the coat hangers from an art installation piece and thrown them at a small table in the chai tea tent as part of an open mic performance. It was a crime and I was an accessory. And at a Christian Festival at that – whatever happened to thou shalt not steal?! Fortunately for her, Christians are also pretty big on forgiveness, although after the reaction our song had received moments earlier you wouldn't have known it.

I was told that she had been sighted later that day returning the coat hangers to the branches one by one. I wish I had seen her positioning them on the tree, then checking with the picture to see if it looked right, then rearranging, over and over again. To be honest, though, putting coat hangers on a tree and calling it art is incredibly pretentious and who among us hasn't seen a work of modern 'art' and not wanted to take it apart and throw it at a table? Sometimes I see works of modern art that wind me up so much I want to go back in time and tell that woman that she's my hero and pledge to back her up at any gig she performs at from now until the closing of the Tate Modern. I once went to the Tate Modern where one of the works of art on display was a mirror. Just a normal mirror. Not even a mirror with a frame. A rectangular mirror. In the Tate Modern. The plaque next to it described the work as 'genius' because the viewer creates the art themselves. If I could've thrown that 'art' at a table and spat all over it while shouting, rather ironically, 'Reflective surfaces!' then I absolutely would have. But as we all know, breaking a mirror is bad luck and I don't know if I need many more scrapes in my life. Although it would help me write a second book.

Anyway, shortly after the gig in the Greenbelt chai tea tent, I decided to commit to doing stand-up comedy. Because after the string of ludicrous bands I had now been in, it actually seemed less stressful and more sensible to get up on my own in front of strangers and try to make them laugh.

Basingstoke

The main reason I started doing stand-up was because I hadn't got any better ideas. The attempts I'd made to continue playing music with people had been disastrous and I'd done stand-up back when I had my mid-life crisis (at eighteen, yes) so thought I might as well do that for a while until I figured out what I really wanted to do with my life. But I quickly became obsessed with stand-up comedy and the open mic circuit (how I was able to do open mic again after Greenbelt I don't know) and found myself trying to get gigs every night of the week almost compulsively. No matter how hard things got I had this urge to get back on stage as soon as possible and give it another go. Even after the somewhat negative experience in Basingstoke that I'm about to relate, I still carried on doing gigs every night.

I had been doing stand-up comedy, unprofessionally, for a couple of months (some people would say that I am still doing stand-up comedy unprofessionally but those people are haters) and as we've already established I accepted any gig offered to me – no matter where the gig was and no matter how much money I lost in the process. This is how I ended up in Andover. I got the cheapest train possible, which meant I arrived in Andover at two o'clock. My stage time was nine o'clock and Andover does not have a cinema.

I really can't stress enough how boring this particular day was. At one point I killed an hour by sitting on a bench. I didn't normally regard sitting on a bench as a leisure activity but in Andover I chose to make an exception. Alongside me on the bench was a big tough-looking gentleman who would shout at people he knew as they walked past. At one point a lady came over and started chatting to him. Midway through the conversation she received a phone call and informed the person on the other end of the phone that she was currently talking to 'Gary and one of his loser mates'. This was hurtful because I had been called both a loser and one of Gary's mates, but what confused me the most was the fact that Gary didn't attempt to correct her. Clearly it was good enough for Gary just to have people believe that strangers were his mates, even if those mates were absolute losers who people slag off openly right in front of them before getting to know them. Weirder still was that when she left, Gary continued to ignore me. But of course he did – I was a loser.

I did have one job I needed to do in the daytime though – I needed to buy a dress. I had written a short film and had roped in a bunch of friends to help me make it and now I was in the process of buying the wardrobe for the cast. I should point out I hadn't made a film before and didn't have the first idea how a film was made. As I said earlier, I was still unsure what I wanted to do with my life and so was trying out all things remotely creative to see what I was capable of. And as it turned out, I was not capable of making a short film. It never got completed and to this day I have no idea where the footage is. We filmed it at the William Knibb Centre (where The Wow! Scenario used to have band practice). We filmed it overnight and while we were there some thieves broke in and stole one of the centre's computers without any of us noticing. Actually, one of the actors did see a robber but wrote them off as a ghost. I wish I was making that up.

I left Gary in charge of the bench and found a little vintage shop full of old clothes, properly FULL of old clothes. The room was extremely tall: clothes hung from the ceiling and stacked up on the floor; sometimes they met in the middle like stalactites and stalagmites (I have lost count of the amount of caves I visited as a child but the only piece of information I have retained from all of those caving tours combined is that stalactites hang from the ceiling, stalagmites come up from the floor and sometimes they meet in the middle. The rest of those tours could've been the tour guide repeating their own PIN number over and over for all I know; I retained none of it).

I had been in the shop for a matter of seconds when a small lady emerged from the dresses. She had unruly grey hair and was wearing a dress that looked much nicer than anything in her shop. She was also far from happy when I told her I wanted to buy a plain red dress.

'All the red ones are really high up,' she said, scowling and pointing to the ceiling. I'm not sure why this was the case and still don't understand the merits of grouping all of the red dresses together in an impossible to reach place. Red seems like a popular colour to me. Keep the red dresses near the door where people can walk straight in and start looking at them and reserve the deepest darkest corners of the ceiling for polka dot shin pads and tweed hot pants, surely? The shopkeeper disappeared, then returned with a long wooden pole with a metal hook on the end and said, 'Which one?' I then had to peer up at the red dress section and point out ones I liked the look of, and then it would take her roughly ten minutes to guide the pole towards the dress, unhook the dress, then bring the dress down safely towards me so I could see it up close and inevitably tell her that it wasn't what I was looking for. She would then have to try and hang the dress back up again, which took longer than bringing it down in the first place. After I rejected the fifth dress I could tell I was testing her patience. I tried to think of an easier way of doing things. Maybe she could hook the back of my shirt with the long pole and hoist me up into the red dress department so I could browse from the rafters and find the perfect outfit while she swung me from one dress to another? I am aware this is impractical and unrealistic but even this idea seemed to make more sense than the current system she had in place.

Once I'd noticed that she was getting irritated I did what I always do and I said yes to the very next option regardless of whether I wanted to or not. This resulted in me leaving with a bright red dress complete with huge shoulder pads. You know, the kind of dress that no one would ever wear ever, even if they were a fictional character in a short film. Excellent work, as per.

Proposed method for retrieving red dresses

I was so relieved when it was time for the gig to start. I didn't know any of the other acts but one of them was giving me a lift home. (The promoter always insisted on there being a driver on every bill who could drive people home if needs be. I had already organised a lift with this act via email, days in advance. I tell you this because later in the story he goes back on his word and screws me over massively and I now hate him and want you to hate him too. I say 'later in the story' but it's literally about to happen next.)

'I've changed my mind,' he said, when the gig had finished. 'I don't feel like going back to London now. I'm kind of shagging this bird in Basingstoke so I'm going there instead.' I didn't have time to ask what 'kind of shagging' meant, instead I immediately checked the train timetables and, of course, there were no more trains to London from Andover. I asked at the bar if I could stay at the pub overnight but was informed that such a thing was out of the question. The bar staff told me that if this horrific scumbag (possibly not their words) was driving to Basingstoke to kind of shag someone then there were trains to London from Basingstoke until midnight and that he should at least drop me off at Basingstoke train station. And so he begrudgingly drove me to Basingstoke train station and spent the whole journey telling me that the Andover audience were shit because they didn't laugh at his Heather Mills routine but did laugh at my routine about bubbles. Now, I had not done a routine about bubbles and have never before or since done a routine about bubbles. I have to concede that I am the sort of act who *would* do a routine about bubbles but that's not the point; the point is that regardless of whether or not I had done a routine about bubbles that night (I hadn't) his message was clear – he was brilliant and I was an insult to the art of stand-up comedy. Did I mention that I hate this man?

Anyway, he dropped me off at the train station at 23:45 and sped off as soon as I had both feet outside of the car. I then looked up and saw that the train station was closed. I tried to get in but all doors were locked. There was no midnight train. There were no more trains until six a.m. I looked in my wallet – no money. I looked at my phone – dead. I looked into my immediate future – bleak. Here are some options that were available to me at the time that have since been pointed out to me by people who are much cleverer than I am:

1) Go to the police station and tell them what has happened – maybe they'll help you out;
2) Go to a nightclub and dance for hours until it shuts;
3) Go to either of these places and ask to charge your phone there so you can ring your auntie who lives in Basingstoke and will definitely let you sleep at hers.

Anyway, that night I slept in a bush.

The amount of time it took me to make this decision was shameful. I had only just established that the station was shut and within a minute I was sitting in a bush right in front of it. It was a big bush, easy to crawl into from the side, and people couldn't really see you from the street. At the time I was convinced I had lucked out with the quality of this bush as it was perfect for sleeping in. I am now somewhat embarrassed by my initial delight as I should really have been more upset, seeing as I was sleeping in a bush in Basingstoke. My delight soon vanished though as reality set in.

I thought it'd be easy to fall asleep and that six hours would pass quickly, but I couldn't fall asleep because I was freezing cold. It had been a very hot day so I hadn't taken a coat out with me but now it was night time, I was only wearing a T-shirt and jeans and I had a problem on my hands.

The amount of time it took me to decide to sleep in the bush was an eternity in comparison to the amount of time it took me to decide to wear the red dress. It wasn't even a decision. I was cold and the dress was warm. I'm no scientist, but if I was I'd be the sort of scientist who sits in a bush while wearing a red dress. Those shoulder pads might not have looked trendy but they were tremendous insulators and I finally felt like the purchase had been a wise one. I made a mental note to start wearing shoulder pads in the winter and not worry about what the old fashion police would say. I became convinced I could make shoulder pads my thing and maybe even bring them back. If I became the shoulder pad guy my whole world could change: I could be a leader, a visionary, people would respect me. These were my thoughts as I sat in a bush wearing a dress, eating brioche and reading a novel (I already had these items in my bag; I did not find them in the bush). I'll admit the whole thing felt a lot more decadent than I had expected, all things considered. I was eating French baked goods and had reading materials to hand, not to mention the killer dress I was sporting. This guy sleeps rough in style. You could even say I was 'sleeping *smooth*'? But you're right, you'd sound stupid if you said that because it's a stupid thing to say.

Even after putting on the red dress I still couldn't sleep because I was too scared. Drunk people were walking past my bush (and it was now *my* bush) and most of them sounded angry. The worst example of this was when two men stood right in front of me, unaware that I was sat at their feet, and expressed to one another how it was a real shame that they hadn't 'beaten the shit out of someone in ages'. I prayed that they didn't look down as I was certain that if they saw me it would feel like Christmas for them. And, by the way, I had no idea that bullies talked like this: 'We haven't beaten the shit out of someone in ages.' So openly, so wistful, just saying how lovely it'd be to hurt someone, for no reason other than how nice it felt to physically abuse another human being. It was quite the eye opener and if anyone ever punches me in the future I will try and remember that for them it's a comforting hobby, an almost romantic pastime, and take some solace in the fact that for one of us at least the whole experience is rather heart-warming. If there's two of them I'll console myself by remembering that they are bonding over the smashing in of my face.

As they debated where the best spot in town was for a good old-fashioned bash-up, I slowly reached for the large plastic bag that the dress had come in and put it over my head so that if they were to look down all they would see was a plastic bag and the dismembered body of a young comedian in a second-hand dress. This is the kind of idea you have at the end of a long day of bad ideas. Go to Andover too early, buy a dress you don't want, trust a man you've never met before, crawl into a bush, put on the dress and put a plastic bag over your head by way of a disguise. I sat there with the bag over my head and stayed as still as possible. Their voices were now muffled; it was just me and my thoughts. And, oh boy, what thoughts they were. I mainly thought about how it was a really good job that I had had a good gig that night because if I hadn't then the entire day would've been awful. I thought about whether or not I should write a routine about bubbles. I thought about what I was doing with my life, how I didn't go to university and instead chose to pursue my passions and wondered whether that had been a mistake. I thought about what I would do if they did attack and decided it would be better to act crazy rather than to fight back or run away, especially because I had never run in a dress before and might not nail it on the first attempt. I thought about who these men were and hoped that one of them would turn out to be

Gary, that way when he tore the bag off of my head to reveal my face he would see that it was I, his loser mate from the bench, and spare me the merciless pounding he was about to deliver; maybe he'd calm down and the two of us could go and sit on a bench for old time's sake, shouting at people as they walked past. And I thought about how long it would take for me to suffocate in a plastic bag and how I should probably take the bag off my head now. When I removed the bag they had gone, my disguise had worked and now those two hoodlums were no doubt beating ten shades out of some other poor sucker who I'm certain wasn't even as easy a target as I was.

I didn't sleep a wink and ended up catching the six a.m. train (sans dress) and getting home shell-shocked and feeling sick from eating too much brioche (I had consumed a whole wheel of custard brioche because I felt so scared of the Basingstoke hoodlums and when I feel scared I eat sweet things to make me feel safe). To this day I have never been back to Andover and I have never forgiven the comedian who didn't give me a lift home that night.

During that first year of stand-up I put myself through a similar experience when I went to the Edinburgh Fringe Festival for the first time. I took a twelve-hour coach journey from Northampton to London to Edinburgh (it was the only route available to me at the time) and then I camped for two weeks in a field twenty minutes outside of the festival by bus. Camping at a festival may not sound odd but the Edinburgh Fringe is not that sort of festival. Everyone else was staying in flats and houses, with central heating and showers; only an idiot would camp for two whole weeks in a *bowl-shaped* field in *Scotland*. It started raining on day one and did not stop the entire time I was there.

That first night my tent got completely flooded, the bowl of a field I'd pitched up in becoming a marshland within seconds. Throughout the fortnight I kept on having to buy new towels to lay underneath my sleeping bag which would keep me dry enough for the night at least. I had found a shop that sold towels pretty cheaply so would go there every day and buy a new towel. The shopkeeper would watch me with suspicion as I walked in, picked up yet another towel without even looking at the design and then paid for it with a handful of change I'd managed to scrape together. *What is this young man doing with these towels that means they never last longer than twenty-four hours?* the shop-keeper would think to herself, *and when would be a good time to cut him off? To tell him he's had enough towels? That his money's no good here?*

In a way this was karma. Karma for forgetting my towel all those years ago in primary school and wiping my soapy hands on Siobhan's coat, and now, eighteen years later, my tent had flooded and towels were the only thing that could save me. True karma would've been to run out of towels or money before the two weeks were up and be forced to use my coat instead of a towel one night, thus receiving a taste of my own medicine once and for all. But somehow I was spared my just desserts and for that I am truly grateful.

Alistair

I was getting a little tired of getting the train from Kettering all the time – arriving in towns way too early, sleeping in bushes, travelling for twelve hours on a coach and camping in the occasional field – so after a year and a half of stand-up, I finally moved to London to at least make the travel side of things a little easier on myself. I love living in London these days but to begin with it took a lot of getting used to.

Most nights I would be doing stand-up but if I ever had a night off I would be overwhelmed with the options available to me in the big city and after choosing an activity, would often mess it up just enough to make myself wish I'd stayed at home.

One evening I went to see the fantastic comedian Mike Wozniak performing his solo show in Islington. I arrived at the venue ten minutes late, rushed in the front door to see the tail end of the queue disappearing into the room where the gig was being held, quickly joined the back of it, paid as I passed through the doorway and sat in the far corner on the back row. Moments after I had sat down the show began unexpectedly with a total blackout. Plunged into darkness, the audience sat still, making no sound for maybe thirty seconds. Then we saw a light. It was coming from a torch but moving in large circles in the air, because it was attached to a rope and someone was swinging it round and round above their head. Every so often the torch would illuminate the person's face on the way past, and oddly they didn't look much like Mike Wozniak. The torch-swinger then started to deliver a loud and eerie monologue about a lighthouse, describing the isolation of the lighthouse keeper and the perils of being a fisherman in a boat out at sea, depending on the lighthouse for your very life. This was a massive departure for Wozniak, who had seemingly ditched his tightly written stand-up routines in favour of mildly upsetting lighthouse trivia. And then the lights came up. There were three people on stage, none of whom were Mike Wozniak, all of whom were dressed as light-house keepers. I then spent an hour watching a play about these three lighthouse keepers who go crazy while cooped up in a lighthouse together and end up turning off the power to the lighthouse causing all the boats to crash into the rocks before they kill themselves. I later learnt that Mike's show had been cancelled months ago.

Sometimes I would simply go out for some drinks with friends in order to avoid such unfortunate mix ups but trouble would befall me all the same.

I am aware that none of the stories in this book make me look remotely good but, fair warning, this one shows me in a particularly bad light.

I was blasted. I've done many things I'm not proud of while blasted. Once when at the Melbourne Comedy Festival, Nish Kumar ate twenty chicken nuggets and everyone made fun of him for it. A couple of days later I got drunk and became convinced that everyone thought Nish was cool for eating twenty chicken nuggets and so I filmed myself also eating twenty chicken nuggets, cussing Nish throughout, fully convinced I had won some sort of competition and was now the best. I completely forgot I'd even done it until I found the video a whole week later, watched it, and immediately felt the urge to exercise.

But I digress (one of the main reasons I wanted to write this book was so I could use the term 'but I digress' at some point and there it is. Do a skydive. Try stand-up comedy. Use the term 'I digress' – life goals getting ticked off on the daily, I ain't never afraid of dying). I had lived in London for a few months and a comedian friend of mine was going through a phase where he made everyone do Jägerbombs whenever we went out, and after one particular night on the town with this stupid idiot I found myself sitting on a London night bus, homeward bound and fully blasted. I was in high spirits, though. I tried talking to the lady next to me about how cool the bus was, but she asked me why I was talking to her and so I turned away to look out the window because I didn't have an answer to her question. (I still don't. I've thought about it since and on a philosophical level I have no idea why any of us speak to anyone else. I haven't done it as much since, actually.) Even though this woman clearly hated me I was still incredibly happy, not so much with myself but just with life. I was in a wonderful mood, and I am hardly ever that sort of drunk. Normally I just go real quiet, a little insecure and go home without saying goodbye to anyone, possibly eating upwards of twenty chicken nuggets in the process. I've been happy-drunk about three times, including this time on the bus. I honestly think getting drunk is one of the most overrated things we do as human beings and yet I keep doing it.

Anyway, I was looking out the window thinking about how being drunk is the best thing we do as human beings when ten lads in their early twenties got on wearing ironed shirts and eating chips. None of them sat down. Instead they spread themselves out around the bottom deck of the bus, shouting across to one another. The leader of the pack was called Alistair. I know this because he shouted, 'What's that Nick? You wanna suck a dick? Hey everyone, Nick here wants to suck a dick!'

And Nick replied, 'Shut up, Alistair.'

And then I said, as a hilarious joke that I was certain everyone on the bus including these lads would find hysterical, 'Yeah Alistair, you wanna watch your mouth.' I am a professional comedian.

When I said, 'Yeah Alistair, you wanna watch your mouth,' all ten of the lads stopped eating their chips and looked at me. There was a pause and then they returned to eating their chips and 'bantering'. I had emerged unscathed and most people in my position would see that as a narrow escape and quit while they're ahead. But then again, most people didn't once sleep in a bush in Basingstoke while wearing a red dress for warmth. My point is, most people are quitters. I had now decided that what would be really funny would be to keep throwing little digs at Alistair after every loud comment he made and to always make sure that the dig included his name. At one point Alistair shouted,

'There's too much sauce on my fucking chips,' and I shouted back, 'Classic Alistair!' I was having a lovely time and being drunk was the best thing ever.

After the sixth dig, the lady sitting next to me turned to me and said, 'You really should shut up.' (This gives you an idea of just how obnoxious I was being. This lady hated me earlier but was now trying to help me out.) To which I responded, 'Why? I'm not afraid of Alistair, he looks about sixteen!'

This, it turned out, was the straw that broke the Alistair's back. He walked over to me and barked, 'What did you just say?'

But if anything this put me in an even better mood, mainly because I had become something of a fan of Alistair and now my hero was finally paying some attention to me, and so I responded affably with a huge grin on my face, 'I said you look about sixteen, Alistair!'

His eyes popped with rage. 'I'll show you who looks sixteen!!!'

'How are you going to do that, though?' I laughed. 'Line up a bunch of kids and be like – he looks sixteen, he looks sixteen but he's seventeen, this one's older than he looks...'

'No I'm going to drag you out of this bus by your fucking teeth, slam your head on the curb, stamp on your eyes...' This latest monologue from Alistair went on for ages. It was graphically violent and I was laughing uncontrollably throughout. I wasn't even laughing in a mean way: Alistair's words were genuinely, in that moment, the most hilarious thing I had ever heard. I laughed so much that one of Alistair's friends put his hand on Alistair's chest and said, 'Alistair, you might want to back off, mate, this guy looks mental,' to which I replied, 'Yeah Alistair, you shouldn't mess with me, I'm from the projects.'

I was particularly proud of the line about being from the

projects so I turned to the lady next to me in order to be congratulated on how funny saying I was from the projects was (I was imagining she'd say something along the lines of, 'I can't believe I asked you why you were talking to me earlier, I know now it's because you're the best, most coolest guy on this planet!') but I received no congratulations because she had gone. Instead of seeing her sitting there laughing because I had claimed to be from the projects, I saw every single one of Alistair's friends looming over me, having formed a sort of horseshoe around me, and looking very much like they wanted to murder me. One boy was blocking my exit by standing with his legs wide apart and holding on to two poles with his hands, like a very cross starfish. As soon

The starfish

as I looked at the starfish he snarled, 'Don't fucking look at me, you face the fucking front.' And so I immediately faced the front and, like that, the spell was broken and I was scared.

They could tell as well. They all started laughing and sneering at me. 'Not so funny now is it?' And instead of sitting there quietly I just responded, 'No it's not very funny any more, actually,' because I still couldn't shut up. I now had to escape somehow, and I'm going to tell you in advance that I *did* escape and I escaped because of the plan *I* came up with. I tell you that because when I tell you what the plan was it will sound ill-advised and stupid and I want you to know going in that it worked.

Here was the plan: I pretended to receive a phone call where I then spoke very loudly, saying, 'Yeah there's about ten of them... Yeah the number 29 bus... about five minutes away... yeah bring him... bring him too...' I was pretending to rally my troops! Of which I had none! Surely the only result I could've reasonably expected here was that they would beat me up there and then before my terrifying gang arrived to defend me! What an unnecessary gamble. This says a lot about me, that when backed into a corner and boozed up enough, I will attempt to bluff my way out of any situation I happen to get myself into. I love a good bluff. The act of winning when you've got absolutely nothing to win with – what a thrill! The only thing more thrilling than bluffing is calling someone's bluff. Taking a chance and accusing someone of lying when they could be telling the truth – what a thrill! If I played poker, all I would do is bluff and call other people's bluff constantly. If you are a regular poker player I probably just blew your socks off with my game-changing tactics so please take a moment to put your socks back on because this scrape is not over yet and I wouldn't want you reading the end with chilly feet.

I sometimes wonder if the lads secretly knew that there was no one on the other end of that phone call. After all I had faked a reaction to the phone ringing on silent and they must've seen it wasn't lit up when I took it out of my pocket. Maybe they knew all along and felt sorry for me so pretended to be concerned that I was calling for backup. I'll never know, but while I was talking to my imaginary death squad, one of the lads asked me who was on the phone and when I didn't tell him, they all started panicking between themselves. This meant they were temporarily distracted when we got to the next stop. I could see the bus doors open behind the angry starfish, and as soon as I heard the beeping noise and they started to close, I leapt like a salmon (that is headfirst with the rest of my body propelling me like one big tail) under his arm then back up into the air towards the door, dodging a kick to the head as I did so, passing sideways through the doors as they shut, landing on the pavement, turning to face the bus and, as it pulled away with all of them looking at me from the inside, I stood in my own starfish pose and taunted them. The perfect picture of a man who has not learned his lesson. At all. I then realised the next bus stop was one minute down the road and instantly ran all the way home, terrified.

But I survived. I slept deeply as one does when blasted then spent the rest of the following day remembering what had happened and feeling sick at how close I came to getting beaten up, or rather obliterated, by ten lads who were all younger than me. Fortunately, I have not behaved like this since. Unfortunately, Alistair and I have not kept in touch. I miss him.

Strimmer

In general though, moving to London had been a positive experience. I had lived in Wood Green in the north of the city for about six months, sharing a house with three very lovely people I had found online, and I was working as a classroom assistant at a secondary school for autistic children in South London.

I loved working at the school. It was an incredible experience and I sometimes wonder if I should have continued working there instead of pursuing a more selfish career path. Not that every day was a picnic, of course. Once I managed to get myself poked in the eye by one of the students. It was my fault: I had said the wrong thing at the wrong time and caused him to feel distressed and so he'd slammed his finger into my eye with the force of a punch and then scratched my eyeball with one of his very long fingernails. I was taken to Moorfields Eye Hospital and while in the waiting room a lady asked me how I'd hurt my eye. I told her the story and at the end she said, 'Oh you work with autistic children! That must be so rewarding!' Yeah... but not *all* the time.

The house I lived in back then was a bit of a mess, mainly because me and a man named Keith weren't tidying anything up. We had a cleaning rota for a while but had to stop using it because the rota itself had gotten too dirty to read.

When we had moved into the house one of the things we agreed to in our contracts was to maintain the upkeep of the back garden. We did not even attempt to honour this agreement. It was a rather sizeable garden and now it looked like a scene from *Jumanji*, overgrown with grass and weeds, a real-life jungle. There could've been animals living in there and we wouldn't have known, and not small animals – a family of stray Alsatians could've been thriving somewhere inside that dense undergrowth and we would've been none the wiser. It got so bad that one of our neighbours snitched us out to the landlord who promptly emailed us saying he would be popping round on Saturday to inspect the house 'in case there's anything you'd like to sort out beforehand'. It doesn't take Alan Turing to decode that email – sort the garden out before the weekend or I'll come down on you like a ton of bricks. We didn't own a lawnmower or any shears, so I decided to ask the headteacher at the school I worked at if there was anything I could borrow from the school, and to my surprise he immediately suggested I borrow the electric strimmer for 'as long as I needed it' and, just like that, all our problems were solved.

I'd never used a strimmer before but I knew this much about

strimming – strimmers were badass. We were sure to have that garden shorn in seconds, probably giving an Alsatian a buzzcut as we did so. The design of a strimmer is so cool as well, it's like a metal detector that makes you feel indestructible. I couldn't wait to rev this beast up and unleash it upon that no good, punk-ass grass back home. They put the strimmer in a bin bag then put another bin bag over the top of it and taped the bags together by wrapping an excessive amount of gaffer tape around the middle. As secure and practical as this was, it did make it look like I was carrying a dead body in some bin bags. I couldn't sit down with it on the tube so just stood by the doors while my fellow passengers looked at me with suspicion, memorising my face just in case I was the most confident serial killer in London and had decided to take the remains of my latest victim home on the Piccadilly line because I was in a bit of a hurry.

I felt terrifically boss returning home with the strimmer. I had saved our bacon. We no longer had to worry about the scary landlord because I would have this garden strimmed in seconds. We hung an extension cord out of the kitchen window (the wide and narrow kitchen window above the main one that's only ever used for running cables through) and I plugged in the mighty strimmer. My flatmates watched from the kitchen window as I carried it over to the haunted forest that used to be our garden. I pressed the on button, half expecting it not to work, and when it hummed into life I was delighted.

I began to to strim.

Back and forth, weeds and grass were disappearing before my very eyes. I felt a sense of pure elation, euphoria even, as I stram with the greatest of ease. For the first time, I understood why people enjoy using power tools. I didn't know if a strimmer technically counted as a power tool, but it was a tool and I'd never felt so powerful. Maybe I'd start doing DIY. I could buy a drill, maybe a sander? I had found my calling and now I was invincible. I turned to look at my housemates, who were celebrating in the window – I was a hero! I raised one hand in the air, throwing rock 'n' roll horns to the sky. As I pulled a series of rock 'n' roll faces to accompany the horns, my housemates' faces changed from delight to expressions of pure horror as they began to frantically point at the strimmer. At first I assumed they were simply getting into the spirit of things and returning my rock 'n' roll gurnings but then I looked down to see that the strimmer's power cord had got wrapped up in the blade and was spinning around wildly, getting shredded in the process. DIY was not my calling. Before I could do anything the strimmer had stram clean through its own power cord, whereupon it stopped strimming and went dead. As soon as it died, all the lights in our house died too. In fact all electrical appliances in the house were now not working because I had tripped the power like a fully certified cool guy.

As I looked at my housemates, all of them standing in a dark kitchen, now shadowy figures who I could tell were less than impressed with me, my main concern wasn't the garden but the strimmer. What would the headteacher say when I told him that within a minute of using it I'd strum right through the power cord and broken the strimmer he had trusted me with? I would clearly have to buy a new one, but how much did these things cost? I'd like you to ask yourself this question now, actually. How much do you think a strimmer costs? I have asked many people this question since this event, and most people guess between £100 and £300. I have checked online and it seems that £150 is about right. But at the time I didn't check online and I didn't ask anyone, I simply assumed, for no particular reason, that strimmers cost around £2,000 each. I did not have two thousand pounds and so I was panicking hard. All weekend I tried to come up with ways that I could raise two grand and pay for a new strimmer. Maybe I could put on a charity car wash with all the money going to me? But we didn't even have the equipment to wash cars with, so I'd have to first of all borrow a bucket, some sponges and a bunch of cloths and whatnot, and then I would undoubtedly manage to break all of those things within seconds. That's how little I believed in myself at this point: I was convinced that I would break a sponge. No one has ever broken a sponge before but I was certain I had what it took to become the first. If I tried the car wash idea I was sure I'd dip a squeegee into some soapy water, touch it to the windscreen and then the whole thing would instantly go up in a ball of flames, resulting in decades of scientific investigation into how this had even been possible.

I travelled to school on the Monday with the strimmer in its bin bags, getting more looks on the tube this time, as not only did it look like I was carrying a dead body in a bin bag but I was clearly riddled with guilt and it was written all over my face that I'd done something I wasn't proud of. Perhaps murder, perhaps damaging a gardening tool that didn't belong to me – my fellow commuters couldn't be sure. When I arrived at the school I headed straight to the headteacher's office and handed him the strimmer, unable to look him in the eye (although he was used to this sort of behaviour as the headteacher of a school for autistic children).

'Did the strimmer work out well for you?' he asked.

I hesitated then answered, 'For a while, yeah.' I looked terribly ashamed of myself and took a deep breath. 'But then I stram straight through the power cord and broke it.' Silence. I was probably about to get fired. 'I'm really sorry, I'll pay for a new one.'

He shrugged nonchalantly, smiling, reassuring. 'Oh not to worry, we'll just get Patrick to fix it,' he chirped and then wished me a pleasant day.

I stood there dazed. This was amazing – what else could I borrow and break? If there were no repercussions I might start borrowing whatever I like, treating it with zero respect and then bringing it back on the Monday for Patrick to fix so I could borrow it again whenever I felt like it. That strimmer cost two grand and he didn't even care! Maybe I could take the school minibus out for a weekend roadtrip, leave it in a John O'Groats car park on fire, text Patrick the coordinates and return to school for Monday morning registration guilt-free.

I later discovered that the strimmer in question barely cost one hundred pounds and that it took Patrick no time at all to replace the power cord. In the meantime, they let me borrow some shears and my housemates and I took it in turns to shear the garden. Shears aren't as fun as a strimmer. For one, they're not as fun a word to say; also for every minute spent strimming you spend an hour shearing and it is impossible to shear without bending over all the time and doing your back in (next time you see someone strimming, note their posture – impeccable). Also, once four people have taken shifts shearing a garden, the level of consistency is all over the shop and the garden will look like it's tried to cut its own hair. I was proud of myself when I returned the shears to the headteacher still intact, although a part of me was tempted to celebrate the completion of the garden by smashing up the shears in the street and then returning the separate parts directly to Patrick, who would inevitably accept that this was going to become a regular thing.

The landlord's inspection went well, though. He walked around the garden, admiring the random tufts of grass, and asked us what we used when mowing the lawn.

'We just use shears usually,' I said and he raised his eyebrows while surveying the scene.

'You should get yourselves a strimmer, they're only cheap.'

Fell Foot Sound

During those early comedy days, I was still in touch with musicians and promoters from my time in the band. One such promoter phoned me up out of the blue to ask me to curate two hours' worth of comedy for a music festival he was setting up called Fell Foot Sound. It would be held in the Fell Foot Woods over four days and on the last day he wanted to put on some comedy around a campfire for whoever wanted to see it. At the time this sounded splendid (these days I know that comedy around a campfire would be an awful idea but that's irrelevant since the whole campfire plan never took place in the end) so I phoned up three of my favourite comedians – David Trent, Chris Boyd and Nathaniel Metcalfe – and booked the full line-up in all of fifteen minutes.

David and I in particular already had a history of bad gigs together. David was a primary schoolteacher at the time and once asked me to come into the school and perform stand-up comedy for the children as part of Red Nose Day.

There were about thirty six-year-olds in the audience and I thought I'd start by asking them if they liked my jumper. They cheered, so I asked them if they liked my green corduroy trousers and they cheered again. Then a kid screamed excitedly, 'What about your shoes?????' and the cheers got even louder, then another kid screamed, 'What about your socks??????' and I pulled the bottoms of my trousers up so they could see my socks and they all fell about laughing. They thought my socks were the funniest thing they'd ever seen. I was wearing plain mustard coloured socks. Then one kid lay on his back and stuck his feet in the air so everyone could see his socks too and all the kids laughed again. Then another kid did it, then another and pretty soon they were all lying on their backs with their feet in the air showing their socks to each other and laughing uncontrollably. So I started describing some of their socks as if I couldn't believe they were wearing them. Stuff like, 'Oh my word!! Blue and white stripy socks! Are you serious?!' One child had gone so far as to take both his shoes off and so I exclaimed, 'He's taken his shoes off!!!!' And then all of them took their shoes off. Then one kid jumped to his feet and started to do a little dance, a combination of the twist and jumping up and down. Then all the kids copied him, all doing the same dance in their socks. One kid got so excited that he jumped as high as he could in the air and then when he landed on the shiny assembly room floor in his socks, he slipped and fully smacked one side of his head on the floor and the sound reverberated all over the room and through my very soul. All the kids started freaking out when this happened. One kid laughed so much that she actually, literally, wet herself, at which point the headteacher ran into the middle of the pit of children, held one hand up at them and another at me and, while looking up at my bemused and helpless face, yelled, 'Enough! That. Is. Enough!'

On the day of the Fell Foot Sound festival, David, Nathaniel, Chris and I decided to travel to the woods in a car together and buy ten big bags of marshmallows to hand out around the campfire. It was a long drive to Yorkshire from London but we were in high spirits and couldn't wait to arrive at a trendy new music festival.

Fell Foot Sound was located right in the heart of the woods. There was a lovely big stage and a friendly, supportive crowd loving every band that played for them that day. Adam, the promoter (the same promoter who'd organised The Wow! Scenario's final gig), had some news for me. 'We've just been told that we have to be done by ten tonight. It's been too loud the past few days so the police have given us a curfew. So...' he pulled an apologetic face that let me know something bad was about to happen '...could you guys do comedy *after* the music has finished instead? That way we can keep the entertainment going.' This didn't sound too bad. As I said, the crowd was friendly and there was a good atmosphere at the festival. We wouldn't be playing the main stage, though; we would be playing on a patch of ground at the bottom of a hill and the audience would all sit on the hill and watch us from above. That also sounded fine. And we weren't allowed to use microphones because of the curfew. And there would be no campfire. Hmm.

It's worth mentioning that no one at the festival was expecting stand-up comedy at all. It hadn't even been advertised when they bought the tickets and wasn't included in the programme. They were also expecting the music to continue until gone midnight, as always.

It was decided that once the final band had played their final song at ten p.m., a nice man called Barry, who actually owned the woods, would walk on to the stage and tell everyone about the comedy. We were told it would be best if the news came from Barry because everyone loved Barry. The previous three nights had all ended with Barry reading a self-penned poem and the crowd had adored him every time.

So once the final band had played their final song, Barry walked onstage and, as promised, everyone went berserk. I've never seen anyone welcomed onstage like it. So much love, birds flying from the trees, people whooping, hollering, whistling, chanting his name: 'Ba-rry! Ba-rry! Ba-rry!' He raised his hands and they quietened down, then one guy shouted from the back, 'Read us a poem, Barry!' And the crowd cheered as one in agreement but, alas, Barry shook his head. 'I can't tonight,' he said. The crowd were distraught. 'Come on, Barry! Read us one of your poems, mate!' 'Please, Barry, Please!' Barry quietened everyone down again. 'Oh no, I can't read a poem you see, because I've got to introduce some comedians, they've come here to do some comedy for you.'

'Tell them to fuck off!', a man shouted.

'We don't want comedy, we want poems!' someone agreed.

'No comedy!'

As one they all started booing and saying, 'No comedy', transforming from an audience into a mob within seconds. I think the comedians were the only people who weren't shouting, 'We don't want any fucking comedy.' Barry raised his hands again, 'OK, OK... ONE poem,' and a mighty roar went up from the crowd. Barry then recited a poem entitled 'Into the Woods' during which he had the entire audience in the palm of his hand. The only line I can remember is 'Into the woods, up to no good', but they couldn't get enough. As soon as he finished the poem they lost their minds anew, totally loco. At one point a guy jumped up from the crowd, crouched beside Barry and pointed at him with both hands while people cheered and clapped like there was no tomorrow. (He looked exactly like the cub scout who double-pointed at Matthew the juggler while dressed as a lion – the exact same pose. This was surely a bad omen.) Barry very humbly accepted the applause and then it was time for the comedy.

As the crowd reluctantly made their way over to the comedy hill I noticed, for the first time, that they were all absolutely wasted, completely trashed and generally hammered. Adam the promoter confirmed that this was the case and informed me that most of them had been doing magic mushrooms for four days straight. I was to be the first act on. Not only was I the first act on but we didn't have a microphone and no one was introducing us. The only thing that made this set up look like anything resembling a gig was that the 'stage area' was lit up by two big sets of lights. They could smell my fear though, because as soon as I stepped out in front of them they began to boo. They booed me ON stage. I was so frightened that I actually brought the ten bags of marshmallows out with me and began throwing them into the audience as if throwing steaks to a pride of angry lions.

The heckling never stopped. Just constant heckling from start to finish. There was one guy sitting on the front, scrawny with long hair and a long beard, who would keep telling me to suck his dick but at a volume that only I could hear so it felt way more menacing and personal than the people shouting about how I was a piece of shit at the top of their lungs. I then introduced the next act.

The next act was the only act I did not book. He was Adam's friend and lived nearby so had been added to the bill. We had met him moments before the gig and David Trent had grilled him in a manner that at the time I had deemed unnecessary.

'What are you going to do, mate?' David had asked him directly.

'About ten minutes of material,' he responded.

'OK,' said David, 'but what are you going to *do*?'

'About ten minutes of material.'

'OK. But what are you going to *do*?'

'About ten minutes of material.'

'OK. *But what are you going to do?*'

This went on for ages, both of them saying the same thing until I told David to stop interrogating this guy and show a little faith in a fellow comic. He was treating him the same way I treated Lloyd before the third Pindrop gig, as if this comedian was about to draw a dick on his forehead and yell at the crowd. I thought David's behaviour had been rather insulting to this poor guy until the unknown act in question walked on stage and uttered his opening line: 'Is it me or are all women lying whores?' Now that line would deservedly get a bad reception at most comedy clubs – even some of the rougher weekend club audiences wouldn't stand for that line – so for him to say that at the end of a festival where they don't like comedians because they think we're all a bunch of piss-taking, narrow-minded bullies, a festival where they had just had an early curfew imposed on them and instead of listening to experimental avant-garde indie music they had to watch their least favourite form of entertainment, a festival where their hero's poetry recital had been cut short because some comedians had taken it upon themselves to close the entire weekend, was suicide. As soon as he said the word 'whores' they went feral. Bottles smashed at his feet, cans whizzed past his squirming torso and a bag of marshmallows smooshed straight into his face and seemed to stick there momentarily before dropping to the ground. They were justifiably angry now. He lasted two minutes then walked off, saying 'Fuck that' to the rest of us and, without stopping, walked straight out of the woods and into his car and drove home. We all looked shocked, apart from David who was feeling pretty vindicated.

None of us got as bad a reception as that guy but we all got the boos and the heckles and we all got the guy in the front telling us to suck his dick. But the guy in the front didn't stop there. During Nathaniel's set he got up and walked around the stage area before approaching David and me. Obviously I feared he was coming over to demand we carry out his request but he didn't; instead he said, 'Can I get up and do some jokes?' This was unexpected and frankly insulting. Clearly we were so bad at comedy that this guy had decided that anyone could do it.

'What are you going to do?' asked David, who was now in charge of screening all strangers before they went onstage.

'I'm going to go up and do a cheer for Barry and then I'll do ten minutes of pure comedy.'

'Ok,' said David, 'but what are you going to *do*?'

I stopped the conversation there and pointed at the guy. 'Absolutely, you're on next,' I said, much to David's confusion.

I took David to one side so I could explain myself to him. 'He's been an arsehole to us the whole show,' I said. 'He deserves whatever happens to him when he tries it for himself.'

As Nathaniel was finishing I asked the guy his name.

'Rybo,' he answered. Of course it was.

I walked back onstage as Nathaniel made his way back to the safe haven otherwise known as offstage, and I made the following announcement. 'People of Fell Foot Sound! It is now time for you to witness the comedic stylings of one of your own! He's been at the festival all weekend! Please give it up for... Rybo!'

Then the unthinkable happened. The crowd lost their minds as if I'd just introduced Barry back on to the stage. They LOVED Rybo. I started to panic. What if Rybo does better than all of us? What if he's way funnier than any of us have been and gets more laughs than all of us put together and he's the one everyone goes home talking about? This wasn't looking good for the Fell Foot Four (a name David, Nathaniel, Chris and I had given ourselves in order to feel braver).

'How's it going, Fell Foot Sound?!' bellowed Rybo, and the crowd went bananas. 'Let's hear it for Barry!' and the crowd went ultra bananas. And then began the ten minutes of 'pure comedy'.

Now, before I tell you what he said I would like to apologise. I hate this part of the story. I really hate it. But it's exactly what he said so, here we go...

'Last night there was a couple in the tent next to me and they were proper getting down to it and at one point I heard the geezer shout...'

I am so, so, so, so sorry for this next line, I considered changing it to something else but this is what he said, oh God I'm so sorry.

'At one point I heard the geezer shout—'

(Sorry, sorry, sorry, sorry...)

'I'm gonna cum in your pussy!'

(I said I was sorry.)

There was silence.

Stunned, horrible, silence from everyone in Fell Foot Woods. It was the first time the woods had been silent in four days. Everyone was staring at Rybo in disbelief and disgust (apart from one guy who looked pretty proud of himself). I slowly approached Rybo and whispered, in a calm voice, 'Come on, Rybo, it's over now.'

He turned to me looking distraught and confused. 'But... but... I thought that'd be funny,' he pleaded.

'I know you did, mate, we've all been there, let's just go now though, eh?'

'Please.' He looked like he was about to cry. 'Please just let me do one more joke. Just one more joke.' Even though it was not a good idea and even though Rybo still hadn't technically even performed ONE joke yet, for some reason I nodded and allowed him to continue because in that moment I actually felt sorry for him. As comedians we were used to tough gigs and had become somewhat immune to the embarrassment that comes with them but this guy had never done this before and wasn't equipped for how it was making him feel. So I gave him another chance. He nodded solemnly back at me in thanks, then raised his arms in the air, turned his back to the crowd and, before I could even take one step away from him, dropped his jeans. Swiftly followed by his underwear. And then he waddled back towards the audience revealing a cold, naked penis. While I was still onstage. The audience were not happy. Not only was a man exposing himself to them but they had nothing to throw at him because they'd used up all their ammo on the misogynist from earlier on. As they booed loudly Rybo looked disorientated once again, this clearly not being the reception he was expecting when dropping trou' in front of an unconsenting audience. So he looked down at his penis, maybe to check it was definitely on display, like maybe he thought he'd accidentally not got his cock out and that's why everyone was so annoyed. Regardless of why he was checking, he did look disappointed when he saw his own genitals. It was a cold night and Rybo's bits and bobs were now rather tiny and the ratios were all off (Chris Boyd, comedian and word-smith, described it as 'ninety per cent bell end'). And so Rybo set about making his penis look more impressive, the only way he knew how.

I had still not left the stage when he began to masturbate. I was frozen to the spot, scared but also fascinated, the whole thing feeling like a surreal dream. The audience protested but Rybo wouldn't listen. He began to shuffle around the stage with his trousers and pants round his ankles, tugging away and shouting, 'I'm gonna cum in your pussy!' I hate to use this phrase a second time but I feel it should be pointed out that Rybo was now employing callbacks into his act, hinting at a higher degree of comedic understanding and professionalism than maybe we had all given him credit for. It's safe to say that I was in way over my head and did not know how to handle this situation. Fortunately for me, a hero was at hand.

Right at the top of the hill a woman sprang to her feet. She was wearing a dog costume and had been wearing this costume all day long. It was beige and fluffy with big floppy ears and a long, shaggy tail. She began sprinting down the hill, towards the stage, her ears flapping in the wind, her eyes fixed firmly on Rybo. Just before she reached the bottom of the hill she jumped, flinging herself towards him, clothes-lining him to the ground. She then pinned his shoulders to the floor with her knees and began to slap him back and forth across the face – forehand, backhand, forehand, backhand – with huge back swings between slaps. In answer to your question, yes, Rybo continued to mastur-bate and yell his now all-too-familiar-yet-still-revolting catchphrase at the top of his voice. And then without warning all of the lights went out and that was the end of the festival.

I mean that, by the way. That was the end of the festival. There was no 'Get home safe everybody', no 'Thanks for coming' – it didn't end with one of Barry's poems or an actual band playing some songs or even some stand-up comedy. The festival ended with a woman dressed as a shaggy dog repeatedly slapping a man on magic mushrooms as he masturbated and shouted obscenities while I stood next to them looking horrified. See you next year, folks.

Twister

After having told a story about a gig that went badly I'd now like to balance things out by telling you the story of a gig that went well, to prove that good gigs can be just as damaging as bad gigs.

I was doing a show in Bath where the promoter provides the acts with free accommodation in a flat right next door to the venue. As the only act who didn't live nearby I would have the flat all to myself that night. My days of sleeping in bushes were behind me; I had free reign of an actual property now – I had made it.

After the gig finished the venue turned into a nightclub, so at the end of the final act's set I was hastily making my way towards the exit door when I was stopped en route by a woman who had turned up as part of a hen party. She said she had enjoyed the night and thought we were all very funny so I instantly liked her. She bought me a drink and we chatted about stand-up for a while. Then she told me that the hen in her group had to kiss a man for every letter of the alphabet depending on what their name began with. She asked me what my name was again (and I told her because I am that free and easy with my personal details).

'Oh cool, she hasn't kissed a J yet!' she said.

'I've got to kiss your friend?' I was clearly not fully on board with this game but then she said, 'You can practise on me if you like.' Full props. I'll admit, up until that point literally no one had ever hit on me before so maybe the line seemed better than it was. Reading it back now, it definitely sounded smoother at the time but then again that line will work on 100 per cent of the single straight men alive today, I promise you.

Her friends came over, took her to one side and they had a conversation while peering over at me from time to time and then she returned with her coat and bag.

'I've got to go,' she said and, maybe because I looked disappointed, she asked, 'What are you doing now?'

'Well, I've got the flat next door...'

She looked angry. 'Oh, do you think I'm that kind of person do you?'

My stomach clenched, I had totally misjudged this and now felt awful. 'Heavens no, not at all, sorry, I shouldn't have said that, if you want my number it'd be great to meet up another time. Sorry.' We swapped numbers, she left and I returned to the flat feeling like a sleazeball.

I was in the flat for five minutes before she rang me. 'I'm outside!' she said.

I opened the door and she ran into the flat and into the living room. As soon as she entered the flat she changed into a completely different person. I followed her into the living room; she turned around and pointed at me. 'Go and get me a Chinese takeaway!' she demanded. I looked taken aback so she reiterated, 'Go and get me a Chinese takeaway now!'

'We can go to a restaurant together if you like?' I tried. 'There should be somewhere open still if you want to get dinner together.'

'No, you have to go and get me a takeaway!'

At this point I started to worry that I was about to get robbed. Maybe this was a trick she regularly played on comics who played the club next door – get invited back, send them out of the flat for Chinese takeaway, then totally fleece the place in their absence.

'I'm not going to go and get you a takeaway, we can order takeaway on the phone if you like and get it delivered?'

'No, you are the man and therefore you have to go out and get me, the woman, a takeaway!'

'Well, I don't think that's true,' I said rather feebly, unsure as to whether the man getting Chinese food for the woman was a thing or not. She folded her arms and sat down, looking grumpy.

'Fine! At least make me a cup of tea,' she said without looking at me. A cup of tea! The perfect middle ground between fetching her a takeaway and not doing anything for her at all. I went into the kitchen, made two teas (obviously paranoid that while I'm in the kitchen she's passing the TV out of the window to the rest of the Hen Do, saying 'There you go, you haven't kissed anything beginning with "T" yet') and when I came back into the living room, she had raided the board game shelf of the flat, had found, and had already set up, Twister. (Strictly not a board game, I know, but I've been to Kettering Board Games Club and there weren't any boards there either so I think Twister still qualifies. Also Twister would be the worst game to bring with you to Kettering Board Games Club. I can't imagine what they would make of it or if anyone would join in and play with you due to the overwhelming amount of physical contact involved.)

She pointed at the Twister mat and quite angrily said, 'We're playing this!'

I was still holding the teas. 'Are you sure?' I asked.

'It's sexy,' she snapped back.

So I set the teas down and we played Twister, just the two of us, with her spinning the spinner *and* playing at the same time (credit where it's due, that's impressive). I don't know if you've ever played two player Twister but it drags on. We were nowhere near each other for the entire game, because all the spinner ever landed on was feet so we were essentially just walking around a Twister mat, occasionally having a swig of tea because we could, and she was getting increasingly frustrated that the game was not as sexy as she'd thought it would be. After half an hour she gave up, threw the spinner on the floor and sat down, declaring that Twister was a stupid game for stupid idiots. Then we had an argument.

The argument started with her making a statement: 'Men are from Mars and Women are from Venus.' I nodded as I was familiar with that term and then she said, deadly serious. 'No. Literally though.' And, like a moron, I took the bait.

'Well, not literally.'

'Yes literally, that's what I believe, what do you believe then?'

'Both from Earth,' I said.

Both from Earth! That's what I once said to someone during

a disagreement – both from Earth! Where are you from, James? Why, I'm from Earth, of course, a man from Earth. This argument went on for longer than I care to remember, and at one point she said, 'Well what about the creation story in the Bible, do you believe in that?'

'No,' I replied.

'Well, I do,' she shot back.

'But you said we were from different planets!'

'I'm allowed to contradict myself!'

'I'm allowed to contradict myself' remains the best line I've ever heard used in an argument because once you've decided that you are allowed to contradict yourself and that you no longer care for the rules of debate then the other person is left utterly helpless, which I was. I was about to tap out when she ended the argument with the line, 'Oh just shut up and run me a bath.' And so I did.

I ran her a bubble bath immediately. I then sat upstairs and reflected on the evening so far. It had not gone well. She had demanded I went out and got her a takeaway, we had played a game of Twister that had somehow ended in a draw, I had defended the fact that human beings were from Earth and she was now in a bubble bath that she had told me to shut up and run for her. But in a typical male way I was also thinking, 'There's still a chance...'

She then walked into the room (not naked, you pervs) and unexpectedly kissed me. I know it sounds ridiculous but it's like she'd changed once more into a different person and no longer hated me or thought that I worked for her and I clearly was so desperate to kiss someone that I wasn't going to say no. There is no way of saying this next bit without sounding like Alan Partridge but... she then raised the question of protection.

I had nothing on me because I had never been in this situation before so wasn't used to leaving the house prepared. She told me that she had seen a twenty-four hour shop across the street that would surely sell what we needed and that I should go there and come back. I agreed in a heartbeat. If the Chinese takeaway order had been a ruse to get to me to leave the flat so she could rob it, I certainly didn't care now. I was clearly happy to risk the entire bounty of the comedian's flat at the faintest possibility of sex. However, when I got to the shop I learnt that it was not twenty-four hours and it was closed. I didn't want to return empty-handed for fear of another argument and also for fear of not sleeping with her. I saw a nightclub in the distance that was clearly open so I decided to go inside and see if they had one of those machines in the toilets.

This nightclub turned out to be very popular and I had to queue up for twenty minutes outside in the cold, only to be turned away at the door because by the time I got to the front of the queue it was closing time. I looked around and saw another nightclub in the distance so I walked there and tried the exact same plan only to achieve the exact same result – queued for twenty minutes, turned away at the door. I had now been out of the flat for forty minutes, maybe fifty. If she was going to case the joint it was done by now; if she was going to have sex with me that was probably done by now too. I had to admit defeat and go home. As I was walking away from the nightclub I began to accidentally walk in tandem with another guy. I don't know why I did this and, even though it worked out well, I will never do it again because it is creepy and borderline insane, but I asked this stranger if he could give me a condom (!!!) and he, against all the odds, handed me an entire pack. It felt kind of gross but at least I had achieved what she had sent me out for. Although technically what she had sent me out for wasn't another man's condoms.

I said thank you to my Good Samaritan but quickly realised my troubles were far from over. I had walked so far from the flat that I now had no idea where I was. I did not own a smart-phone at the time so couldn't access maps. I was simply lost. I finally get myself into a position where I'm getting accommo-dation provided for me after gigs and it's looking like I'm going to end up sleeping in a bush again. I didn't even have a red dress on me this time; I would have to stretch a full pack of condoms over my arms, heads and legs to provide me with any insulation. How had I allowed this to happen?

I took a guess and walked in what I thought was the general direction of the flat, quickly lost faith after ten minutes and so made my way down a different road that just 'felt right'. At this point I had been out of the flat for an hour and I was in a right tizz. That tizz only got worse when I heard the rushing of feet gradually getting louder behind me. I looked up to find myself surrounded by about fourteen teenagers. There was a pause as I waited to get mugged, desperately scanning their faces in case Alistair and the boys had finally tracked me down and I was about to get my just desserts. Just when I thought the kicking was about to commence they all started jumping up and down, clapping their hands and singing a song. The song went: 'Olly Bongo, Olly-Olly Bongo, Olly Bongo, Olly-Olly Bongo' over and over again forever. This was one of the most surreal moments of my life. I still don't know why it happened. All I know is it wasn't what I hoped I would be doing by that point in the evening. Eventually they stopped singing and then ran off into the night,

I assume to sing the 'Olly Bongo' song at some other bewildered boy who'd been out begging strangers for contraceptives.

I didn't realise it at the time but having those boys sing the 'Olly Bongo' song at me was actually as nice as my evening was going to get. There's no nice end to this story. The truth is I returned back to the flat, she told me she wasn't in the mood any more (there's not a person on the earth who would be in the mood any more, let's face it) and so I went to sleep and was awoken a couple of hours later by her leaving. When I asked her why she told me not to be such a baby.

But let's look at the positives. She didn't rob the flat, I got a lovely song sang to me by a late-night flash mob, and after a quick online search I'm proud to say that I was right – women and men are both from Earth.

I'd like to say I learned my lesson but there was another occasion where I went back to somebody's place with them and the next morning as I was leaving her flat I was unexpectedly chased down the street by a white Highland terrier wearing a pink T-shirt that said 'I Heart Bones' on it. All in all, I am glad to not be in my twenties any more.

Mr Eko

Doing all of these disaster gigs while working at the school was exhausting but I only had to do it for nine months. One day when walking back to the tube from work (probably carrying a hedge trimmer that I intended to drop from a twelfth storey window before returning it to Patrick the following morning) I received a phone call from one of my favourite comedians (and one of the reasons I became a comedian) Josie Long, asking me to be her tour support that autumn. Being her tour support meant that I would have to quit my job at the school because I would essentially be on the road for four months. This was great news. Even if I ended up having to return to the day job once the tour was over I was still incredibly grateful for any respite whatsoever. I said yes without hesitation.

The tour began in September and I was one of two support acts. The other was Johnny Lynch, an incredible musician who releases music under the name The Pictish Trail. The tour started in the Scottish Highlands and I remember driving over the hills, looking down at rivers and realising that it was one o'clock in the afternoon and I'd usually be working in a class-room by now, and it made me feel free and fortunate. (I know some of you are thinking, 'Woah should you really be the one driving given your track record?' But relax, I'm hardly going to mar this amazing experience by having my third major car crash, guys!)

The tour ended in Nottingham and I was very happy because my sister and brother-in-law were going to come to the show. I had arranged to meet them for a drink before the show started but I wouldn't be eating food because Josie, Johnny and I had decided to go and get some Italian food together when I got back. Ruth and David (my sister and brother-in-law's names) were waiting for me in Chiquito's (the name of the restaurant we were having drinks in). We sat at the bar and had drinks and caught up with each other for about an hour before my sister spotted Mr Eko sitting on his own at a table.

Mr Eko was a character in the popular television series *Lost*. All three of us were fans of *Lost* and probably even bigger fans of Mr Eko. He was a Ugandan drug lord turned preacher who was sitting in the tail section of the plane when it crashed and did loads of spiritual stuff on the island as well as beating people up. And Ruth was right: Mr Eko was sat at a table alone, waiting for his order and drumming on the table top. I never approach people I'm a fan of for fear of annoying them but I loved his character in *Lost* so much that I just had to say something. So

I walked right up to Mr Eko and said, 'Hello, mate, just wanted to say you're amazing in *Lost*.'

He smiled and said, 'Aw thanks, that really means a lot,' shook my hand, and I returned to the bar. It had been a success; I had met a hero and not come across like a weirdo. I was happy.

After the drinks I returned to the venue to meet up with Johnny and Josie. I was hungry and it was dinner time. 'We're going to Chiquito's,' said Josie.

I froze. 'Ummm... I can't go to Chiquito's.'

'Yes you can,' said Josie, looking puzzled.

'No. No, we can't go to Chiquito's, I've just gone up to a man and told him I love him and then left, I can't return five minutes later with more people, he'll think something's going on.' I tried explaining the situation to Josie and Johnny more coherently but they didn't see the problem (which is totally fair enough) so in the end we reached a compromise. I agreed to eat at Chiquito's providing Josie lent me her hoody and Johnny lent me his bobble hat thus providing me with the perfect disguise. Genius.

And so we arrived at Chiquito's and waited to be seated. I was now disguised as the coldest person in the world, wearing a hoodie with the hood up, bobble hat on top of the hood, and blending in with the Mexican decor very nicely. Mr Eko was still sitting at the same table, checking his phone.

'There's one table free at the moment,' said the waiter and of course pointed straight at the table right next to Mr Eko.

'No we can't sit there,' I whispered to Josie, 'Mr Eko is literally on the table beside us.' This was not a good enough reason to not sit at the table for reasons I don't have to explain to you because you are a reasonable person who knows that that is not a good enough reason for anything ever.

I sat with my back to Mr Eko as we waited for our food and refused to remove my hoodie or bobble hat. My chimichanga arrived but before I could start eating, Mr Eko got up to leave. I know that Mr Eko got up to leave because in order to get out he had to squeeze past me and asked me to move my chair so that he could get past. I was so startled that I pulled my chair forwards too quickly, sharply knocking into my table which caused my fork to fall on the ground. And then Mr Eko and myself both bent down to pick up the fork at the same time, and whilst under the table our eyes met. I froze in fear; he did a double take, recognised me and a look of concern swept over his face as he asked himself why this man had gone away and then come back wearing a disguise and sat on the adjacent table to him. In a way it's rather fitting that someone from the TV series *Lost* should suddenly find themselves with so many questions but zero answers. Now they know how we felt.

When I saw his eyes widen I realised that what I'd done was so much worse than if I'd simply returned to the restaurant dressed in the same clothes as earlier and had a meal without bothering him. This looked suspicious. This looked like I actually had something sinister planned. I had gone to the trouble of disguising myself, concealing my identity from him. Whatever I was about to do next would most certainly be illegal and probably unwelcome. He thrust the handle of the fork into my hand and left hastily, looking over his shoulder at me as he did so.

And then I ate a chimichanga while wearing a bobble hat.

But even though the Mr Eko situation hadn't panned out as I'd hoped I was fairly relaxed about it, mainly because it was, by an awfully huge margin, not the worst thing that had happened to me during the tour.

Déjà vu, Déjà vu

It was about a month before Mr Eko-gate and we had just started the Welsh leg of the tour. We'd done Swansea the previous night and in the morning we drove to Brecon to meet some friends for lunch before setting off to Machynlleth for our next show. The drive from Brecon to Machynlleth was going to be a scenic one, winding through Welsh hillside and through areas of woodland. The promoter had met up with us in Brecon and he was leading the way in his car with us following him in ours. We stopped at a big Tesco early on and I bought CeeLo Green's album *The Lady Killer* for £4.99 just so we could listen to the song 'Fuck You' in the car. We then proceeded to listen to it about a hundred times during the journey. Over and over again, singing along, really loud. It's the perfect song to listen to when driving through beautiful scenic countryside. Fuck You, wildlife. Fuck You.

At one point we got stuck behind a lorry carrying about 80–100 logs, trundling along for quite a while until it signalled for us to overtake. The promoter in the car in front of us was able to do so but we didn't think we could pull it off in time so we stayed put. This left us in a tricky position because we didn't know the way to the venue without the promoter and had no way of contacting him because we had no phone signal up in the hills. So for about twenty minutes we trailed behind the log lorry, occasionally peering round to see if we could overtake and agreeing with each other that we could not. After twenty minutes of this we reached a very long, very empty stretch of road that we all unanimously agreed we could overtake the lorry on without any problems occurring.

As we began to overtake I was surprised that the car wasn't accelerating as fast as I was used to. What I haven't mentioned is that this was the second hire car we'd had on the tour. The first one had been pretty nippy, but this was only the second day we'd had this new car and it was far from nippy and right now its lack of nip was causing me to worry as we crawled alongside the lorry. We were getting closer and closer to the bend and it didn't look like we were going to make it past the lorry in time. By the time we approached the corner we still hadn't cleared the cab of the lorry and I found myself hoping with every inch of me that the road would remain clear round the bend, but instead four cars came round the corner head on with ours. Everything else happened very quickly and I only know what took place because our poor friend the promoter saw everything unfold in his rear view mirror (he'd stopped to allow us to catch up and had unwittingly parked up in a spot that gave him the perfect view of the upcoming catastrophe).

I steered in between the cars and the lorry, somehow keeping from hitting anything, and as we came out of the corner I had managed to get in front of the lorry and hadn't hit a single car. But then I caught the front of the very last car with the back corner of mine and span in front of the lorry. The lorry then ploughed into the passenger side of our car, pushing us down the road, then pushing us off of the road up a grass verge on the right hand side, then through a garden, demolishing a greenhouse, then back on to the road again, causing the lorry to drive over the front of our car, obscuring our friend's view of us completely. At this point the lorry flipped over and all of the logs came loose and rolled off the lorry and on to our car. The car was then carried amongst a swirling sea of rolling logs, some of which were embedding themselves in the windscreen, before we burst through a hedgerow and into a field where we finally stopped moving. The only means of escape was Josie's passenger window, which we all clambered out of, jogging over several waves of logs to safety. All three of us stood in the field, looking at the scene, in a daze.

The lorry driver couldn't come over to us because all of the logs were in the way. His lorry was in the road on its side and he'd only got out because two men had just pulled his entire windscreen off and helped him down from his chair.

'Who's the driver?' he called to us, politely and calmly with concern in his voice.

'I am,' I answered, meekly.

'You're a fucking wanker, mate!!!'

Yeah, fair play, I'd be angry too; just can't believe I fell for the old 'who's the driver' trick. That was very crafty pretending to be concerned about my wellbeing then calling me a wanker. Nicely done. I looked down at my hand and saw that I had saved the CeeLo Green album from the wreckage without thinking. I also had 'Fuck You' in my head still. We'd sung it so many times that it was now playing on a loop in my brain and it didn't go away until the next day. The whole time the police were questioning us about the crash I had that damn song in my head and was worried I would accidentally start to sing or hum it with them still within earshot.

Just in case you're wondering how many car crash stories are in this book, don't worry, that is the final one. I only had one more near-death experience involving a car, some years later when I had just finished a tour show in Norwich. My friend and tour support Stuart Laws and I got into his car and it refused to start. Eventually Stuart phoned his breakdown company and I went off to buy us some curries to cheer him up. By the time I returned the recovery service man had got the car started but had some instructions for us before we departed. 'This car will not start again so you must not turn this engine off before you get to where you're going.' This was a problem because we only had enough petrol to get us one minute outside of Norwich. When we told the man this he told us we would have to put petrol in the car WHILE THE MOTOR WAS STILL RUNNING. He then led us to a petrol station and stuck around while Stuart filled up the car without turning the engine off. I was worried that the entire petrol station would explode and so to avoid getting hurt I walked to the edge of the forecourt and ate my curry from a 'safe' distance. I think my main concern was that I'd chosen a hotter curry than usual and a three-pepper-heat curry might just be the extra catalyst this situation didn't need. As I ate the curry on the edge of the forecourt watching Stuart bring the nozzle towards his car, I thought to myself, *How amazing would it be if after being ridiculously lucky in a car crash that involved a log lorry, I end up going like this. Blown up by my own curry reacting with some volatile petrol while my friend attempts to refuel a running vehicle.* But, once again, I somehow made it.

After the car crash, the Welsh gigs were cancelled and I returned to Kettering via train. And here's a nice little PS to the story: on the way home my train nearly derailed because it hit a falling log. Obviously I like to think it was one of the logs from the log lorry and it'd been rolling constantly ever since the train crash, seeking me out so it could finish the job.

The train shook for a while, then stopped abruptly and then they made an announcement telling us what had happened. But I already knew we'd nearly derailed because I knew what being on a train while it was derailing felt like. Because it had happened to me before.

Derailed

In February of that year I had travelled from London to Leicester with my good friend and colleague Josh Widdicombe. Josh is a great guy and was just coming out of a phase where he forced people to drink Jägerbombs every time they hit the town with him.

Before we'd even left London I remember a young man approaching us. Josh and I were sitting opposite each other on a table for four, the other two seats were empty, and this young man walked up to us with a long cardboard tube under his arm, clearly wanting a chat.

'All right, lads?'

It was actually quite refreshing to have a stranger say hello; it doesn't happen enough nowadays. I personally only ever speak to strangers when I'm trying to score condoms off of them. But there was still something a little off about the way he sidled up to us, and he clearly had an agenda.

'I've just been to London!' he said proudly, which was an odd statement to make because the train left from London and we were still very much in London, therefore one could safely assume that everybody on the train had just been to London. 'Guess what I was doing there?' We didn't know. 'I was giving a talk on wind energy! I work for a charity, I was trying to get some investors!' Then he opened the cardboard tube and pulled out a poster that featured loads of pictures of windmills and said, 'What do you think about that?'

We nodded approvingly. 'Pretty good,' we said.

'You can get loads of wind energy out of them!' he beamed, and we raised our eyebrows as if we didn't know that already. 'Yeah well this is what I've been talking to people about so fingers crossed!' There was an awkward pause and then he went, 'Well, see ya later!' then gathered up his poster and sat the other side of the aisle directly across from us. He was a good guy and I love the fact that he said 'see ya later' then sat down right next to us.

For an hour there was no problem with the train journey whatsoever. Then there was a sudden jolt and some mild shaking. Then rocks started to fly out from underneath the train. Then the shaking got more intense and the rocks flew higher. Then the rocks started arching over the train and some of them started hitting the train itself and smashing the windows. Then the whole train began to shake extremely vigorously and everyone fell silent. I remember Josh and I both held on to the table with both hands and looked at each other as the train shook and the windows smashed. And then everything stopped. The train stopped moving and we let go.

For a while no one knew what was happening. We were all trying to guess what'd gone wrong. Naturally our friend in wind energy came over to us (by came over to us I mean he stood up and turned to face us) to hazard a guess at what had happened. He kept asking if we had GPS on our phones, as if the train had somehow gone the wrong way and we'd got lost. He was midway through dispensing some bonus wind farm trivia when an announcement was made over the speakers in the carriage. 'Hello. Just had a bit of problem... basically the wheels of the train that keep us on the tracks... they've fallen out... they've just fallen off... But don't worry... the train is *not* on fire...' None of us had even asked if the train was on fire! No one was worried about the train being on fire before he said it wasn't on fire! As soon as he said we are not on fire, all I could think about was that we were definitely on fire! It was at that moment that a lot of us realised we could hear the fire alarm in the background of his announcement. He continued, '... there is, however, an awful lot of hot oil spewing on to a hot axle.' Oh great. That sounds bad. Spewing is never good, is it? No one has ever delighted in discovering a spewing something. Take any noun and put spewing before it and it instantly becomes worse, I guarantee it.

So what do you do in order to keep everyone calm if you've got an awful lot of hot oil *spewing* on to a hot axle? Answer – send a lady down the aisle of every single carriage with a packet of Tangfastics. Fizzy gelatin-based sweets. That was the solution. Josh and I were sat right at the end of the carriage so we knew all the good ones would have been snapped up by the time it got to us. We were getting cola bottles and we knew it.

The lady with the Tangfastics stopped near us and looked at a smashed window, pointed at it and asked us, 'When did that happen?' As if she knew nothing about the derailing and was just handing out Tangfastics because she had some going spare. Maybe she thought the wind energy man had got so carried away talking about wind energy that he had attempted to smash all the windows, thus allowing wind to rush freely through the carriage in order to illustrate his point even further. I like picturing him stood on a table, wind whooshing through the smashed glass, shouting, 'Think of the benefits!!!!'

We were stationary for three hours while we waited for a rescue train to arrive. And by the time said rescue train arrived it was very dark. This meant the train staff weren't legally allowed to evacuate us without the fire brigade present so we had to wait another hour for the fire brigade to arrive. And once the fire brigade had arrived, the train staff and the firemen had an hour-long disagreement about what side of the train to evacuate us on. And then, after five hours of sitting on a broken train, we were ready to get on to the rescue train that had arrived two hours ago. I know – bloody red tape.

The firemen were standing in two lines facing each other. The lines started either side of the door to our train and led round to the door of the rescue train. All the firemen were pointing their torches at the ground so we could follow the path of light to safety. While I was walking along the path of light, one patch of torchlight suddenly disappeared and shone on the face of another fireman.

'Phil? Is that you? I didn't know you were in today!' said the fireman holding the torch.

'Yeah, got called in last minute,' said Phil, blinking in the light.

I'll be honest, I didn't find this easily distracted fireman in the slightest bit reassuring. If they all started recognising the person standing opposite them I'd be lost in a blizzard of moving torch-light and probably stumble into a badger sett and twist up my ankle. So I stepped over the patch of darkness where his light used to be, just to be on the safe side.

On board the rescue train the buffet carriage was free and everyone was taking full advantage of it. One of the saddest sights I have ever witnessed is a man getting himself a free can of Stella from the rescue train buffet; then turning round and holding it up to his wife, who was sat at the far end of the carriage, and silently celebrating with the can as if everything had now been worth it. The five-hour delay and being involved in a derailing had all paid off because he had managed to get a single can of free lager out of the whole ordeal. This attitude only exists in Great Britain. We will forgive all manners of inconvenience if we end up with some free food and drink at the end, especially if it's booze. We're the first to complain and yet the easiest to trick out of formally complaining. Personally, I stocked up on marble cake and never contacted the train company asking for a refund.

Paris

After the car crash in Wales we took some time off from the tour. Josie cancelled the Welsh leg and we all recuperated separately for about a week before resuming the tour again, in Paris of all places. Johnny was unable to come so the plan was and for just Josie and I to do one gig, stay in a hotel overnight and then go home. We arrived early in the day so that we could take in as much of the city as possible (because I treat Paris the same way I treat Andover.)

One of my biggest phobias in life (number two actually, just underneath singing in public) is trying to speak other languages. Every time I try and speak another language in another country I completely freeze up and lose confidence and feel dreadful. When we were in France, I relied on Josie at every turn. Josie definitely seemed to enjoy speaking French more than I did and people understood her much more than they understood me when I mumbled something vaguely French to them in a Kettering accent. I clung to her all day long and was left alone once for about seven minutes, during which time I managed to mess up in a way that surprised even myself.

Josie wanted to look in an 'everything for a euro' shop but instead of browsing along with her I opted to wait outside like a cool kid. I was not alone, however, for next to me there was a big dog. The big dog looked like a six foot man in a dog costume tied to a post and was looking happily at everyone who walked past. I think the lady who dressed as a dog at the Fell Foot Sound festival had been paying homage to this actual dog, that's how much it looked like a human in fancy dress. It had big shaggy white hair and a fringe that covered its eyes. It looked hilarious, no two ways about it. Everyone who went past that dog laughed out loud. One or two people would laugh at the dog and then make a comment, in French, to me about the dog, in a manner that made me suspect they thought the dog belonged to me. Every time this happened I would laugh back, nod and say 'Oui' because I had no idea what was being said to me but I knew that I agreed the dog was the funniest dog in all of France so 'Oui' seemed like a pretty safe bet.

One guy could not get enough of the big dog. He stopped, did a double take, laughed, walked away, returned again, pointing, laughing, looking up at me and gesturing towards the dog in disbelief, shaking his head, grinning constantly, completely agog. He then said a bunch of stuff to me about the dog while pointing at it so I did my stock response and laughed and said 'Oui'. As

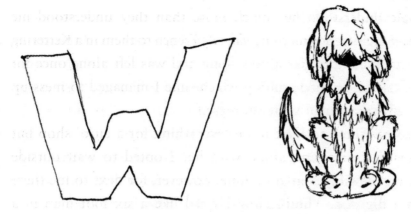

The size of the French dog compared to a yellow W

I said 'Oui' a passing lady stopped in her tracks and narrowed her eyes at me and the laughing man. She looked appalled. The laughing man stopped laughing and returned her glare with a look that said *What's your problem?* And then she launched into a full-on angry rant in French, all of which was aimed directly at the two of us, including loads of finger-wagging and head-shaking, sometimes pointing at the big dog then back to us again with more ferocity than before.

What on earth had I agreed to? This man seemed harmless enough but I suddenly started to fear that I had just agreed to either eating or, worse still, having sex with the big dog. I know that's disgusting but that's where your mind goes when you're currently being scolded in a foreign language and have no idea what for. You instantly think you must've condoned bestiality out loud on the streets of Paris. And if this man was the sort of awful human being who suggests such things to strangers he now felt well and truly emboldened because as far as he was concerned he had found himself an ally. He was no longer alone. I suspect that usually he suggests these taboo ideas to total strangers and they tell him to get lost but today he had found someone as laid back and unorthodox as he was, a kindred spirit, and this angry lady could get stuffed if she's not on board. Throughout the bollocking he would look over at me and roll his eyes, gesturing towards the woman with his thumb as if to say, 'She doesn't get us, man.' This had always been my biggest fear when it came to speaking another language, saying the wrong thing and then the situation quickly escalating into something I didn't understand. All I had said was 'Oui'. That's the first word you learn in French class and it had landed me in a world of *merde* (the second word you learn in French class).

I kept looking back at the shop hoping that Josie would return but there was no sign of her. There must've been so many amazing things available for one euro in that shop and she was lost among the glorious bargains. Maybe she'd found Ceelo Green's entire back catalogue in there for just one euro and was buying it for me as a present. Or maybe I was just telling myself that to distract from the fact I was about to be put on some sort of French register. The angry lady was still telling us off and showing no signs of stopping so my partner in crime made a dismissive gesture towards her and walked away, leaving me to receive the remainder of the dressing down on my own. Eventually she stopped yelling, maybe deciding there was no point now that the ringleader was gone and I was clearly a good kid who'd just fallen in with the wrong crowd. So she shook her head at me, looked at the big dog (I swear she nearly laughed when she looked at it; even after all that angry shouting the sight of that dog was still funny) and stomped off down the street. It was at this point that an old woman emerged from the euro shop, untied the dog and walked off with it. Then, once the big dog had completely disappeared from view, Josie also emerged from the shop and I had to tell her what had happened in the few minutes since she'd last seen me, despite the fact that all of the key characters were nowhere to be seen. I left out my theories about what I thought the man had said to me for fear of sounding ridiculous but once I'd finished the story, Josie thought about it, nodded and said, 'He probably said, "You and me should bang this dog."' It was nice to feel understood again.

I would like to point out that I like dogs and would never do anything to harm one even out of awkward politeness due to a misunderstanding with a Frenchman. In fact, growing up, my family owned a miniature sausage dog and one day I saved its life.

I used to own a green and white puffer jacket. It was my favourite jacket and I received many a compliment on it. One day I had returned home from school, taken the jacket off and thrown it on the floor before practising the drums for an hour. During drum practice I paused to hear wheezing coming from the living room. I popped my head in to investigate and saw that the family sausage dog had crawled into one of the arms of my puffer jacket and was now stuck with her head sticking out the end where the hand would be and her tail pointing out the other like an antenna. She clearly was not enjoying the experience and was having trouble breathing so I went to get her out of the puffer. But as soon as I tried to reach inside I realised two things. The first was that in her panic she had urinated all over the jacket and the second was that the jacket had now formed a vacuum seal around her body and it was impossible to get my fingers inside in order to pull her out of there.

Her wheezing got louder and so I had to think fast. I ran into the kitchen, grabbed a pair of scissors from the drawer, ran back

A sausage dog stuck in the sleeve of a discarded jacket

into the living room and cut her out of the jacket without hesitation. OK, there was a moment of hesitation where I thought, *Hold on, this is my favourite jacket* but I knew I couldn't risk it and decided the puffer jacket and I had had a good run. Farewell my green and white friend, family comes first.

As soon as she was free my dog skipped away without seeming either grateful or relieved, just frolicked off like nothing had happened. When my family returned home I recounted the tale to them, expecting to be declared a hero and receive adulation and gratitude for saving the family pet. Instead they told me that I probably overreacted and my mum was disappointed that I'd thrown my coat on the floor instead of hanging it up. And so, as revenge, I decided to bide my time and then, when she was least expecting it, I ate all of her wild strawberries (I can't even joke about that actually. Oh man, I still feel awful about gulping them.)

Alcatraz

Shortly after Josie's tour ended, I managed to secure the tour support for another favourite comic of mine, Milton Jones. Surprisingly, Milton's tour contained no scrapes. The most crazy it ever got was when I dropped an open yoghurt on the floor of the dressing room and Milton got some yoghurt on his shoe.

All in all I had a lovely time; such a lovely time, in fact, that as soon as it was over I immediately left the country. I hadn't been able to afford a holiday in years but while supporting Milton, I saved enough up to be able to go to San Francisco and stay in a hostel for ten days on my own.

I'd never stayed in a hostel before and I wasn't entirely sold on my room mates, one of which was a guy who had brought a lady back one night and 'done it' in the bunk above me. This was doubly annoying because it wasn't even his bunk. He had moved beds in order to disturb me in the worst way possible. As if knowing someone's in the bunk below is one of his major turn ons and since there was no one in the bunk below him that night his options were to move onto the bunk above me or to ask me if I wouldn't mind moving onto the bunk below his for the duration of the shagging. He chose the nicer option of the two but still, not a fan.

I ended the holiday with a trip to the world famous maximum security prison, Alcatraz. I had to book the Alcatraz trip in advance because it was so popular and I looked forward to it the whole holiday. I'm sure you're aware that in order to get to Alcatraz you have to take a ferry because it's on an island. The ferry journey itself was nice and relaxing, until I idly looked inside my wallet to see that all of my cards were missing. All of them. Someone had taken the cards but left the cash. I had just been pickpocketed and yet *I* was the one heading directly to jail. Not. Fair. I was freaking out. We were now halfway to Alcatraz so I could hardly ask them to turn the ferry around. I was trapped, so I began to pace around the top deck like a madman, willing the ferry to hurry up and get there, the other passengers all looking at me thinking, *Well, he is really looking forward to going to Alcatraz, that limey can barely contain himself.*

As soon as we arrived at the prison I ran to a nearby help desk. I only had a pay-as-you-go phone, with no internet, so I didn't know the number to call in order to cancel my cards. I needed help.

'You've got to help me,' I pleaded. 'My credit cards have been stolen.'

The lady behind the desk looked perplexed. As far as she was concerned this British tourist clearly believed that if you get mugged in San Francisco the first thing you've got to do is report directly to Alcatraz. For all she knew I could've been mugged in London then got straight on a plane and flown here, determined to take this all the way to the top. I saw the confusion in her face.

'I just need to use your phone so I can cancel my credit cards,' I clarified.

She looked apologetic. 'I'm sorry, you can't, this phone is for staff use only.'

OK. A few problems with this. For starters, I've just arrived at a prison, therefore I'm entitled to a phone call. I've seen enough American films to know the system over there. Also, this is Alcatraz and I was trying to catch a criminal, so they should be the first people to rush to my aid. The guards who used to work there back when it was a fully functioning prison would be appalled to learn that these days the employees were allowing pickpockets to run amok through the streets of San Fran, refusing the victims access to the staff phone. I tried to convince this lady to let me use the phone but she refused time and time again. We actually argued for so long that by the time I gave up, the ferry had returned back to the mainland. I was stranded and, of all the islands to be stranded on, Alcatraz was probably the hardest to leave. I was trapped on an island that has been specifically designed to contain people. The few people who have apparently escaped Alcatraz were never found and were thought to have died while trying to swim to freedom. The next ferry would not arrive for another forty-five minutes, so in the meantime I took the audio tour.

The Alcatraz audio tour is narrated by ex-prison guards and

ex-prisoners of Alcatraz. I think it's safe to say I was not in the best head space to be taking this particular audio tour. Every time a prisoner was describing how tough it was to be incarcerated on Alcatraz I was so happy, walking around in front of the other tourists saying stuff like 'Good!' out loud and snickering at their pain. The ex-guards would talk about the punishments dished out to the murderers but I was like, 'Hurry up and get to the pickpockets! Tell me what horrors awaited them! The very worst I hope! I do hope you didn't spare the pickpockets!' Other visitors would've seen me nodding my approval at the size of the tiny cells and testing the strength of the bars, pulling them until I was satisfied that no two-bit crook was going to bend them any time soon. Fantasizing about throwing the staff at the ironically named Alcatraz Help Desk into one of these babies, have them do a long stretch for assisting and enabling a common thief and being traitors to the spirit of Alcatraz itself. Maybe I'd throw all the staff in prison and become the new Alcatraz prison warden and clean up this goddamn city once and for all. I'd soon have this beautiful jail chock-full of criminals once more and I'd reserve a cell in the darkest, dankest reaches of the building for the sonuvabitch who lifted my credit cards and give him a bunkmate who would have sexual intercourse on the bunk above him all night long (by this point I'd decided that the thief was definitely the sex guy from the hostel). And if Alcatraz ever shut down again and went back to being a tourist attraction then I, the ex-warden, could narrate the audio tour and I'd make it a lot more hardcore than the tame-ass one I was currently listening to. I'd send out a message to all filthy criminal punks, pure and simple: 'just because this prison is closed does not mean I won't still hunt you down and destroy everything you hold dear you scum sucking vermin.

Remember my name – and not just because it's written on the credit cards that you stole, which I'd like back by the way. Seriously, just give me back my credits cards you arseholes, what is your problem? You've ruined my friggin' holiday! I hate you! T-shirts are available in the giftshop, thank you for visiting Alcatraz.'

The tour is meant to take an hour but I obviously had to rattle through it in order to catch the ferry in time. You can and should spend hours on Alcatraz. I don't think anyone before me has ever arrived on one ferry and left on the very next one. I boarded, absolutely livid. I was certain the cards had been stolen by the man who had done sex on the bunk above me the night before and if I hurried back to the hostel I would surely be able to catch him before he made his getaway.

I arrived at the hostel and realised I could use the payphone in order to cancel my cards. I went upstairs into my locker to retrieve my bag which contained some loose change, and what should I find there but all of my credit cards which at some point had somehow fallen out of my wallet and into my bag. My own mess-iness had caused me to ruin my entire trip to Alcatraz. The real crime here was poor organisation and the criminal was none other than yours truly. I rethought my future contribution to the Alcatraz audio commentary. 'Guys, sometimes it's possible to lose things by accident instead of being a victim of actual crime so I implore you all to check your pockets several times and consider all possi-bilities before you go spoiling your visit to one of the world's most fascinating and informative tourist attractions. That being said, the people who work at the Help Desk here are still fully certified dicks so feel free to flip them off from me on your way out and tell them to "suck it" as your ferry's pulling away. T-shirts are available in the giftshop, thank you for visiting Alcatraz.'

Wine

I was now living in a different Wood Green house with a group of friends I had known since before starting comedy. It was a terrific house to live in because everyone was very social and would often organise fun nights out, or nights in, together. My housemate Daniel was once bought a private wine tasting by his sister as a birthday present. A sommelier would be coming to the house to talk him through a series of fancy wines and all of his housemates were invited too. There were six of us there, eight if you count the sommelier and his apprentice, and we quickly learned that when you invite a stranger into your house and allow them to hold court it inevitably makes for quite the awkward atmos. It also became clear that the whole thing was a sales pitch in order to get us to buy the wines. We had naïvely assumed that paying for the experience of the wine tasting would be enough. But paying for the wine tasting was the furthest thing from enough. The whole tasting was one big pressure sell and he tried to get us to buy the wines by telling little stories with each demonstration. Every single story was about a different time him and his mate Jim had got absolutely blasted. The stories got gradually more and more debauched until we all stopped laughing at them and instead reacted with concern because the man seemed like he might have had a serious problem. The stories that weren't concerning were a little on the dull side.

One story was about how he had rung Jim up and told him he'd got a bottle of that wine he likes, so Jim told him to come over to the hotel he was staying at and bring some cheese. So the sommelier went into a cheese shop and bought a whole wheel of blue cheese, then went to Jim's hotel where they put the cheese on a radiator so it was nice and soft and ate it with spoons that the hotel owners had allowed them to get from the kitchen themselves because they knew them so well.

The thing is, when he originally told that us story I was twenty-six and thought it was boring but just now as I wrote it out for you I have to admit that sounds like the best thing ever. I'm thirty-two now and, as a thirty-two year old, sitting in a hotel eating a wheel of blue cheese from a radiator with spoons I've selected myself from the kitchen because the staff know me, staying up late and sharing an expensive bottle of quality wine with my best friend, sounds like my ideal evening, and I genuinely wish I was doing it right now. If you told me that story today, as a thirty-two year old, I would buy the wine from you immediately, get the name of the cheese and buy that too, then grab a spoon, crank up the heat and head to my nearest radiator.

Every time we tasted the wine he would ask us what flavours we were getting. Our answer, always, was 'wine flavour', as we had no idea. He would then tell us what flavours we should be getting (none of which we could detect – he could've said anything he wanted and we would've acted like we could taste it) and at one point he said, 'You should be getting a hint of... do you remember those French sweets, Campinos? You should be getting a hint of that.' Campinos were a strawberries and cream flavour boiled sweet that I hadn't eaten since I was thirteen on a school trip to Boulogne. He said, 'I bet you're kicking yourselves now you didn't guess that one.' We weren't kicking ourselves; I was hardly going to start guessing artificially flavoured sweets in order to appear sophisticated ('I'm detecting a whiff of Jolly Ranchers, anybody else? Exquisite!').

It then came to the part of the night where he asked us, 'So – who wants to buy some of the wine I've shown you today?' I felt like I was back at the French porcelain exhibition. Come to think of it, a lot of these wines were French also. Maybe this was a common French sales tactic – do a presentation that appears not to be a sales pitch and then put them in an awkward position at the end and ask them if they want to buy all the things they've politely agreed were nice. Maybe that was what the man in Paris said to me regarding the dog. Maybe he was starting a sales pitch that would eventually lead to me having to buy the dog but the lady overheard and decided she'd had enough of pressure selling so gave us both a piece of her mind. God, I hope that's what happened.

The sommelier stood with his arms open, looking around at us for an answer.

'Sorry, we don't really have any money,' the birthday boy said.

Well. The wine man threw a right strop. He moodily repacked all the wine into the hamper he'd brought it in, while his apprentice looked at us apologetically.

'Sorry,' my friend tried as the wine bottles bashed against each other in the boxes.

The man didn't even look over. 'No, no...' he muttered, 'who cares, you got your free taste.' He was right actually: on the plus side, we had got a free taste.

It took quite a long time for him to pack up all of his stuff so we just had to sit there and watch as he angrily repacked his wine tasting equipment and occasionally threw us glances or muttered 'waste of my time' under his breath. When he eventually did leave we were all a bit stressed so we unwound with a £5 bottle of wine we'd previously bought from Morrison's. It tasted of Wine Gums.

Badminton

While living in North London I regularly played badminton with my friend Sam. Sam used to play squash for Northamptonshire and I hadn't played any sports since I was thirteen when I was in a rugby team. The rugby team I had been in was a good one though. I joined the team when I was ten and we won every single game we played until we all turned thirteen and all the thirteen year olds in the whole country had a growth spurt except for us. We were now going up against fully grown adults who were shaving as they walked on to the pitch; we lost every single game we played and found out the hard way that we had an awful lot of 'cryers' on the team. Fastforward to my late twenties and I'm losing every single game of badminton to Sam but holding the tears back and being a brave, brave boy.

Sam and I arrived on the badminton court one evening and, as we started to play, two women came in and started a game on the court next us. After five minutes one of them walked over, stood on our court while we were in the middle of a rally and said, 'DOUBLES!' It was a little forceful but we accepted because we didn't seem to have a choice and because they were worse at badminton than I was.

'Boys versus girls,' the woman said, ushering Sam over to the same side of the net as me. 'Boys versus girls' made me fear we were about to enter into a 'men are from Mars, women are from Venus' argument instead of a badminton match, most likely resulting in Sam and I standing on our side of the net shouting 'from Earth!' until our voices got hoarse. But to my relief we started playing badminton and about two minutes into the game two men walked in, also holding badminton rackets. The men stopped in their tracks when they saw us playing badminton and stared in disbelief. I noticed their faces and concluded that these guys must've been mighty impressed with how much we were thrashing these ladies and then one of them stepped forward and said to one of the women, 'What's all this?'

She looked back at him, angrily. 'You were late! If you're late this is what happens, we find some other men and they play with us instead!'

Now as far as badminton players go, these men looked pretty gangster. They were way stronger than me and Sam, and I feared we were about to enter into another doubles game and one we would most certainly lose (because that game of doubles would be an actual fight with fists and kicking, not a badminton match with rackets and a shuttlecock).[6] Although, I was quite flattered that the ladies referred to Sam and I as 'other men', as compared to these guys we did not look like we qualified. One of them actually had a full beard that he'd shaved patterns into.

At this point in the story, I'd like to point out that every time I went to play badminton there was a child at the leisure centre who would bully me. He was six years old, tops, and someone had clearly updated this kid about what adults are scared of these days, because every time I was in the changing rooms getting changed he would burst in with two different friends every week and point at me and laugh. His timing was amazing because it's like he knew when I was about to put my shorts on. I'd hear him outside giggling his way up the corridor, which meant I had to rush and pull my shorts up really quick. I'd get them on just in time before he burst in and absolutely killed himself laughing. This kid laughed like an actual cartoon character, both hands on his stomach, rolling around the floor on his back and kicking his legs in the air with unparalleled glee. I know I could've just changed into my shorts before I left my house or worn shorts underneath my trousers but it was a long journey to the leisure centre and I had to go by tube. I didn't want to expose my nobbly knees to my fellow passengers because I'm very self-conscious about my nobbly knees. I also didn't want to stand there with an oddly big butt because I've got secret shorts on underneath a pair of cords.

Anyway, this kid did this to me every week and would then run up to the viewing gallery and laugh at me from there while

---

6   Haha, shuttlecock.

I was playing badminton on the court below. Sometimes he'd even run downstairs and somehow sneak up behind me without me knowing and when I turned and saw him he would kill himself laughing again and scamper away. I could only imagine what a nightmare this little sod was to kids his own age considering how effortlessly he bullied a man more than twenty years older than him. Relentlessly tormenting this innocent badminton novice with all the confidence of someone with ties to the mob. I'm still scared that when he grows up he'll track me down and pick up where he left off just for the sport of it. Man, I hated that kid.

So we're playing doubles against two ladies and two angry men have shown up and are wondering why the women aren't playing against them like they promised and in the end the ladies say to them, 'Look, you can play the winner, how's that?' and they agreed. We didn't seem to have a say in the matter. We did not want to play these men but we were already winning by a significant margin against these ladies. I then did my best to throw the match. Sam, however, is naturally competitive and so continued to wipe the floor with them. The men began giving the women advice during the game, on two occasions initiating some sort of huddle where they discussed our weak points (although we only had one weak point and that weak point was me). We (Sam) still ended up winning the game and so had to play these angry men who seemed to think they now had something to prove. And we (Sam) thrashed them even easier than we'd thrashed the two women who may or may not have been their girlfriends but whose approval clearly meant a great deal to these particular guys. We were playing a blinder.

At one point I looked up at the gallery to see the kid who

bullies me looking very disappointed indeed – it was all I could do to not shout up at him, 'Yes! Are you watching this, you Satan?! You Devil?! Behold!' At the end of the game I did half expect to be beaten up by the two men we'd just humiliated. They were peeved to say the least. Their badminton date hadn't panned out the way they'd hoped and they hadn't been in the slightest bit friendly to Team Sames from the word go (yes, Team Sames is Team Sam and James). But instead of pulverizing us they shook our hands and left with the two women who were smirking at them all the way out of the leisure centre. And then Sam beat me three games in a row and that little kid returned to running up the walls with laughter every time I got hit between the eyes with a shuttlecock.[7]

---

7   Haha, shuttlecock.

Xmas Tree

People don't talk about this enough, but buying your first Christmas tree as an adult is a significant moment in your life. And buying your first *real* Christmas tree as an adult somehow feels even more significant. I think this is because, like all adult decisions, it makes zero sense. You know you'll be hoovering up pine needles until the following Christmas but you've decided it's worth it for the house to feel two per cent more festive than it would with a plastic tree. But once you've got one you instantly regret it and day after day you're reminded that it's not even remotely worth the hassle. This is how I also feel about pensions, mortgages and water filters.

After the second Wood Green house I had moved into a tiny flat with my then-girlfriend near Camden. There wasn't much room for a tree in there but it was our first Christmas in the flat and we felt like making the effort. When moving in together we both had to be very selective about what we brought in with us in terms of personal belongings due to the limited space. This resulted in a long and heated argument over Andrei Kanchelskis. An argument which I lost because, bottom line, bringing a human sized toy alligator complete with neon pink top hat and party gator t-shirt into a flat that can barely contain the two human sized humans who live there is never going to happen[8]. It is still one of the most ridiculous arguments I've ever had, mainly because no matter how angrily you say it, 'party gator' is not a phrase that can ever be taken seriously. To give you an idea of the size of the flat, it was so small that the bedroom linked on to the living room via a sliding frosted glass door because there wasn't enough room on either side for a door that opened outwards. One time, my then-girlfriend (as I will be referring to her throughout this entire story) woke up in the middle of the night and in her tiredness tried to open the slide door like a normal door by pulling it towards her and it broke and jammed itself between the floor and the door frame. This meant it blocked the entire doorway and was impossible to squeeze through. I attempted to move it back into place and the glass let out a mighty creak that sounded like it was about to break and I immediately got scared and stopped trying to move it. We were three floors up but there was a chance we could phone a friend (albeit at four in the morning) and get them to come and stand

---

8 I managed to re-home AK with the friends who had found the W in Northampton. They still have him to this day and he has since acquired a prom queen sash. He's loving life.

outside where we could throw them our keys and they could let themselves in and move the glass door from the other side. Except we couldn't do that because our keys were in the living room. I tried to move the door again and it made that same awful noise. My then-girlfriend really needed to go to the bathroom and we were running out of ideas so we phoned the fire brigade. This is the only time I have ever had to call the emergency services, which is a surprise considering some of the events that take place in this book.

The lady on the other end didn't sound hugely convinced but took our word for it that this was indeed an emergency and said someone would be on their way soon. What was really great was that she sent out the five firemen who most found our situation utterly hilarious. The ease with which they sorted the door out was embarrassing but then again they were wearing protective clothing so weren't as scared of the glass breaking and slicing them up. What stuck with me the most was the comment the first fireman made when he climbed in through our bedroom window. 'Jeez,' he said. 'It's a bit hot in here isn't it?'

This was a comment that every visitor to our tiny flat made because it was indeed always hot, but when you consider that most of the buildings this man enters are on fire, I think that's pretty rich. A bit hot! Compared to the flames you're usually wading through? A bit hot is it? Compared to an inferno? A bit hot? The nerve of that fireman. They were unable to get the door back on its dollies so it just became one of those things you have lying around in the house. Just a huge glass door, propped up against the wall next to an empty doorway because of that time we'd trapped ourselves in our own bedroom and had to call the fire brigade to get us out.

So now we had decided to buy a tree, if only to distract ourselves from the ever-present dead door that we couldn't use.

There was a supermarket on my street that was selling proper, real-life Christmas trees. They were all on the pavement out front and today was the day I was finally going to purchase one.

When I got there all of the trees were looking pretty sorry for themselves, and there was only one good one left. It looked beefy, it looked healthy, it had volume, and it would be mine. So I picked it up and made my way into the supermarket so I could buy it. I headed straight for the tills, which annoyingly were the other side of the supermarket, meaning I had to negotiate the aisles on my way there. Weaving in between other shoppers while holding a big Christmas tree is hard. I was shedding needles all over the place and stumbling between trolleys and toddlers, constantly trying to keep an eye on the top of the tree in case it wiped out an entire shelf of tinned goods in one careless swoop. I felt a tap on the shoulder and turned to find one of the supermarket employees looking at me with a worried expression.

'You're not supposed to bring them inside,' he said.

I froze. When you think you're *supposed* to walk around a supermarket with a Christmas tree you feel pretty cool and maybe even admired by your fellow shoppers. When you're *not supposed* to be walking around a supermarket with a Christmas tree you feel somewhat exposed when standing in the middle of the supermarket holding a Christmas tree. It's like having a dream when you're suddenly naked in public.

'There's a barcode tag on the top, you just bring *that* in and leave the tree on the pavement,' he continued, pointing at the top of the tree where the aforementioned barcode tag hung like a star. Well, this made perfect sense. What did I think was going to happen? When I got to the tills what was my plan? To lay the tree on the conveyor belt and pop a next customer please sign after it? Maybe chance my luck on the self-service checkouts and weigh it on the scales, choosing the Christmas tree option from the menu? I made my way back outside, following my own trail of needles like Hansel and Gretel, then I put the tree down, removed the tag and walked with ease to the tills.

Once I had paid for the tree I went back outside to discover that it had vanished. All the scrawny trees were still there but where was mine? I looked up and down the street and then finally back into the supermarket where I could see the top of a healthy looking Christmas tree, without a barcode tag hanging from it, bobbing up and down above the biscuit aisle. I headed back inside.

For a while I was having to stand on my tiptoes to see over the aisle shelves in order to find the thief. They were very tricksy, weaving in and out of various aisles (trying to shake me no doubt), but I didn't give up and it wasn't long before I'd cornered my foe in the frozen food section. It was a dad with his two young children. The kids were probably five and eight, at a guess – y'know, the age where Christmas is the best thing in the whole world – and they looked very taken with their new tree. But this was my tree, this was my *first* tree, my first tree as an adult, my first real tree. I couldn't return empty-handed.

'Excuse me, sorry but that's actually my tree.' I was very polite and spoke softly and with an understanding tone. If his kids hadn't been there this man would've immediately told me to fuck off, but instead he said, 'Well it's not your tree is it because I've got it.' Dammit. His argument made perfect sense. Then he pointed at a lasagne ready-meal in his trolley. 'I suppose that lasagne is yours as well, is it?'

'No, just the tree. I've already paid for the tree, you see,' I explained.

'Is that a fact?' he scoffed, then pointed inside his trolley. 'I suppose you've already paid for that lasagne as well.'

'No I haven't,' was the best response I could come up with because I really hadn't already paid for the lasagne and don't know why I would've wanted to. I needed to explain the system to him. 'You see, what you're meant to do is remove the barcode from the top of the tree, then go inside the supermarket, pay for the tree using the barcode and go outside to collect the tree afterwards,' I said.

The man raised his eyebrows then picked up the lasagne, looked at the back of it and said, 'Sorry, just checking in case you'd stolen the barcode off the back of this lasagne as well.' The man's obsession with his lasagne was infuriating. But I was not going to allow myself to be sidetracked. I knew what he was doing; he was trying to move the argument on to something else so I'd get distracted and forget about the tree. But I wasn't falling for that old trick.

This went on for a while, and every time I tried to explain the system to this man he would shift focus on to the lasagne. I've never known anything like it. A lasagne is nothing like a Christmas tree. They fit inside a trolley easily, they don't shed parts on the way to the tills, they can be easily shelved, and all ready-made lasagnes are the same – there aren't good ones and bad ones like with natural, real-life Christmas trees. You cannot compare a Christmas tree and a lasagne. But this man found about fifty different ways to compare the two as if they were the most interchangeable things on the entire planet. The amount of times I had to say, 'No sir, I haven't bought that lasagne' was ludicrous. I shouldn't really have needed to say it *once*, let alone repeatedly.

In the end, the same supermarket employee who'd explained the barcodes to me approached us and calmed the man down. The man actually listened this time and didn't once rebut with any accusations regarding his lasagne. Once he understood what had happened he reluctantly handed over the tree. And as I accepted the tree I made the mistake of making eye contact with his children. When I saw their sad little faces, it just didn't feel Christmassy of me to rob them of their tree, even though it was technically my tree. Christmas itself belongs to children, not adults, so maybe this tree was rightfully theirs more than it was mine.

But of course I did not give it back because my then-girlfriend had given me the job of buying the tree that day and I didn't want to fail at the one job I had been given so bad luck kids, your dad should've learned the rules before grabbing trees willy-nilly. Merry Christmas. And then I stole his lasagne (I didn't steal his lasagne but I wish I had done).

Another significant Christmas for me was the first Christmas when I bought other people presents. I would have been maybe eight or nine years old and told my dad that I was tired of giving people presents bought by my parents but with 'from James' written on the tag. He was cool about it and when I set off to do my Christmas shopping he had just one thing to say to me: 'Remember, you're buying presents for other people so don't go out and buy yourself any presents today. Christmas is about thinking of others, OK?'

I nodded and set off to buy everyone some top-notch presents: a bar of soap for my mum, a chocolate bar for my brother, a chocolate bar for my sister and a chocolate bar for my dad. And then I spotted it – the best song I had ever heard had been released on cassette single: 'I'd Like To Teach The World To Sing' by No Way Sis. No Way Sis were an Oasis parody band who dressed and sounded like Oasis. No Way Sis had taken it upon themselves to do a cover of 'I'd Like To Teach The World To Sing' because Oasis had done a little nod to that song during their track 'Shakermaker'.

I wanted that single badly. It was £3.50 and I had spent less than £2 on each of my family's gifts. But as far as I was concerned, no one would ever know. I could keep the single a secret for a while, I was sure of that. It's not like wiping your soapy hands on someone's coat. There's no streaky hand marks left behind when you buy yourself a present illegally (illegal according to the Christmas rules, that is). I'd just buy it then keep it hidden for a month or so then start listening to it when there weren't as many eyes on me – foolproof! I got home and craftily stashed the No Way Sis single in a separate bag to everyone else's gifts. I hid the cassette along with my dad's present in my bedroom and gave the rest of the presents to my dad for him to hide.

Ten minutes later my father called me into his room and when I entered he was holding a small piece of paper and looking quite serious. 'This is a receipt, James, it's a record of one of the things you bought today.'

What?! I began to tremble. He allowed this information to sink in then looked back at the receipt. 'Thing is, the item written on this receipt doesn't appear to be in your bag. Tell me, what is No Way Sis?'

I had not foreseen this. I'd never bothered to read what was printed on a receipt; how could this double-crossing-piece-of-snitch-paper betray me like this? My dad had followed the paper trail and rumbled me in seconds!

'Um... Let me think...' I stalled unconvincingly. But he didn't wait for me to 'think' at all.

'It also says you spent more on No Way Sis than on anything else you bought today.' It says the price too?! This receipt was singing like a canary!!! I hadn't encountered such a little telltale since Simon sold me out in primary school.

'That... might... be... for me,' I caved.

He slowly breathed in and out, a look of disappointment on his face, and then sat down.

'So. I asked you not to buy anything for yourself today and not only did you buy yourself a gift but you spent more on your own gift than on anyone else's?'

I sat down opposite him, the reality of the situation dawning on me. I then reacted like a murderer confessing his sins to a priest. I put my head in my hands, shaking my head, and said, with the greatest despair and the deepest regret, 'Oh God. What have I done?' My dad was looking at me now, trying to ascertain whether I meant what I was saying or not, so I went further. 'I would give anything to take it back,' I sighed, secretly hoping he would let me keep it.

But he knew just what to do to relieve my guilt. 'It's OK, why don't I just buy it from you now and you can use the money to go and buy more presents for other people instead?'

I paused and tried to look thoughtful. He'd really backed me into a corner here. 'Not... necessarily...' I attempted before my father persisted.

'You said you'd do anything to take it back,' he reminded me.

I nodded. 'I may have misspoken,' I said, trying my best to act like someone who had learned his lesson but somehow still deserved to reap the benefits of what he'd done wrong in the first place. But there was no getting out of this because, let's face it, my dad's proposal was the most reasonable thing I'd ever heard.

I didn't see the No Way Sis single again until my birthday on 9 January. My dad had wrapped it up and given it to me as a surprise present. I have never felt so guilty when opening a gift. Happy Birthday, James, you selfish little oik.

New Year's Eve

But the scrapes don't end at Christmas; I've had some pretty shoddy New Year's Eves too. One time, I drank too many Spicy Peppers (spiced rum and Dr Pepper) and then didn't stop being sick for hours. At one point all I had done in 2013 was puke. I have never drunk Spicy Peppers ever again, not that they have ever been offered to me by anyone because a) I made them up myself and b) they taste revolting. If I ever become a wine sommelier and go from house to house trying to sell people wine in their living rooms, my main story in between tastings will be the cautionary tale of the Spicy Peppers. I'll use it as a way of scaring the customer into drinking only wine from now on. After all, no one has ever sat next to a radiator and enjoyed a rare Spicy Pepper while eating the finest soft cheese with a spoon they picked out themselves from the hotel kitchen. If you make a move towards the hotel kitchen with a Spicy Pepper in your hand you will be escorted off the premises and sent packing and on the way home you will be sick on the London Underground five times (in my experience).

My worst New Year's Eve had occurred a few years earlier when I had done my first (and only) New Year's Eve gig. The gig was in Gloucester and my friend George had accompanied me as he didn't want to spend another New Year's just getting trashed in the same old pubs back home, so came along for a change of scenery if nothing else. I had not paid attention to all/any of the emails I had received about the gig and was unaware that I would be performing in a church and the audience would be the church's regular congregation. I found this out when I arrived at the venue and walked in to the sounds of a Christian rock band doing their soundcheck. I reassured myself that this was not a disaster. I'd played to Christian crowds before, back when I was in that short-lived experimental jam band with a lady who played the coathangers, and from what I remember they were a broad-minded sort of audience, open to almost anything. If I could get some chai tea circulating and source about a dozen or so coathangers, I could give these people what they wanted.

A man greeted me at the door and briefly explained how the night would work. 'So what's going to happen is this. The vicar will go on and talk about Jesus and then he'll introduce a boy who goes to the church to play "Blackbird" on the acoustic guitar while all the parents wipe away tears because they all know how far the boy has come over the years, not just as a musician but as a child of God, and then the vicar will return to the stage without a microphone and will mumble your introduction so people won't really know you're a comedian and you'll walk on to confused applause and then you will die on your arse for forty-five minutes and you'll come off and your friend George will look at you and tell you that the experience of watching you tank in front of these people was nothing less than brutal and then a Christian rock band will go on and everyone will get up and dance.'

Those may not have been his exact words but that's precisely what happened. As soon as I came offstage and George told me how brutal it had felt to see me suffer like that, we left. We had to catch a train in ten minutes or else we couldn't get home and we had no accommodation sorted in Gloucester.

So once we'd missed the train and were stranded in Gloucester for the night we took some time to consider our options. When I had missed the train in Basingstoke it was pretty easy to immediately crawl into a bush because I was the only person who needed convincing of my own awful plan. However, when you've got another person in tow it's extremely difficult to talk them round to your way of thinking and have them agree to join you in a bush for the night, both wearing matching dresses, tearing and sharing brioche like there's no tomorrow and welcoming in the New Year with plastic bags over your heads so the bullies can't see you.

As we walked aimlessly around Gloucester, asking pubs to let us in only to be told it was 'ticket only' tonight, it gradually dawned on us that we would have to go back to the church and ask if one of the nice Christian people would put us up for the night. It wasn't ideal – these people had just seen me die quite the death. On the plus side, Christians love a good resurrection.

So back we went, safe in the knowledge that as Christians they were contractually obliged to show us kindness and mercy and give us shelter for the evening. And that they did. A very kind and very merciful family put us up for the night. They were lovely. I stayed in the spare room and George slept on the pull-out bed in the family office.

The next morning we had breakfast with the nice family before leaving. I asked the dad what he did for a living.

'I'm a GP,' he replied, while buttering his toast.

George pointed at him. 'I knew you were a doctor,' he declared confidently, 'because before I went to sleep last night I was looking through your letter rack in the office and I found a photo of a breast.'

There was a long pause, then the doctor went, 'Hmmm,' and then we absolutely had to leave. On the train home I asked George if he thought it had been a good idea to tell the doctor that he had found a photo of a breast while rooting around in his letter rack and George, to his credit, defended himself by saying, 'It wasn't that rude, I could've said tit.'

Fancy Dress

When I was six I was invited to a *Teenage Mutant Ninja Turtles* themed party. My friend Elijah had invited me and when I told him I didn't have a Ninja Turtles outfit and that the only fancy dress costume I owned was a Superman outfit, he told me that would be fine and just to wear that instead. You might think it'd be a little bit embarrassing to be the only person dressed as Superman at a Ninja Turtles party but what's more embarrassing is being the only person dressed as Superman at a party where no one else is in fancy dress, which is exactly what happened to me. And yes, I know this is pretty much the exact plot of an *Only Fools and Horses* episode but instead of Batman it's Superman and instead of a wake it's a birthday, but this really happened to me, a long time before that episode was ever on television as well, years in fact. For all I know, the writer of that episode of *Fools and Horses* was one of the mums and dads at the party and as soon as I walked in a light bulb went off above their head, a few tweaks and they'd got themselves one of the all time-classics.

Unlike Del Boy and Rodney, I took this unfortunate situation completely in my stride. I just mingled as I had always intended to, all the other kids dressed normally, me as Superman. I could've taken my cape off but then I would've looked somehow stranger, so I stuck with the full get-up. I looked like one of those kids who wakes up in the morning and their parents let them wear whatever they please in order to express themselves, but in actual fact I'd just been lied to by my best friend for no reason. I didn't even get made fun of, because Elijah didn't even reference it when he saw me. Sure, a few kids had some questions but when I told them that I had been lied to by the host they just accepted it. They weren't outraged or surprised, they didn't find it funny, just a matter-of-fact conversation:

'Why are you dressed as Superman?'

'Elijah told me it was fancy dress but it wasn't.'

'Cool, I'm drinking lemonade.'

Oh to be six again. If I turned up to a party dressed as Superman as an adult people would be incredulous, they'd be telling me to go home and change, they wouldn't be able to have a serious conversation with me, I'd be made to feel so self-conscious about my choice of attire that I wouldn't be able to enjoy the party. But when I was six, apart from one kid who flipped my cape in the air and ran away, everyone just let me get on with it. Obviously what I should've done was fly around the world backwards so that we all went back in time and I could turn up at the party dressed like everybody else, but hindsight is a wonderful thing.

Fancy dress parties never got any better for me either. Jump forwards to Halloween 2014 and I had been invited to a proper fancy dress party where everyone would be in fancy dress and the host wasn't a six-year-old or a compulsive liar. It was the party of some new friends; however, I also had to do a gig that night and wasn't able to sort myself out with a costume in time. I was told not to worry because there would be a rack of costumes at the door for anyone not in fancy dress. Perfect. That way, if this was another trick then I wouldn't turn up in fancy dress only to discover everyone in their normal clothes and then have to be a pariah all night long. Fool me once etc.

And so I did my gig then travelled to the flat in North London.

When the door opened I saw that the place was absolutely rammed but couldn't see anyone I knew, and everyone seemed to be about ten years younger than I was. I later learned that my friends were in a different room and these younger guests were friends of the host's sister.

The door was answered by a twenty-year-old male dressed as a skeleton. What was particularly noteworthy about this skeleton was that it had a scar painted across its forehead. This was the first sign that this guy was bad news. You can't be a skeleton AND have a scar, it's one or the other. You can have a crack in the bone or a hole in the skull but a scar makes zero sense. Pick a team. Still, maybe he was a nice guy and I was just judging him on his outfit.

He took one look at me, pointed at me with a can of beer in his hand and said, 'No costume, fuck off home.' I was right; he was a nobhead.

I laughed because I assumed he was just doing a bold joke. 'I understand there should be some spare costumes lying around?' I said.

He then plucked a costume from the rack next to the door, held it out to me and said, 'Put this on, this is what fucktards wear.'

I'd never been called a fucktard before. He wasn't smiling or joking either; he just aggressively called me a fucktard while handing me a red onesie that had a rubber wolf mask stapled to the hood, with a crown glued to the wolf's head to top it all off. I had not seen an outfit like this before but I knew immediately what a look like this must be known as. King Wolf. I was to be King Wolf, which would've been fine but I'd also be a fucktard since 'this is what fucktards wear.' I decided to clarify the situation.

'I'm sorry, did you just call me a fucktard?' I asked.

'Yes I did, just deal with it, fucktard,' was his response.

I began to suspect that the scar on his forehead wasn't fake after all and he'd once tried this shtick with a much bigger much stronger person who didn't hesitate to lamp him in his stupid handsome face (credit where it's due, he was pretty handsome).

There were some young women standing near the door, so I turned to them and asked who this boy was, and they told me he was my friend's sister's boyfriend.

'He's horrible,' I whispered to them and they looked at me like I was the horrible one, rolled their eyes and walked away.

He turned to face me again. 'Grin and bear it and put on the costume, fucktard.' This guy really liked calling me a fucktard.

Now I've got a dilemma on my hands because on the one hand I want to get into the party and find my friends but on the other hand if I put on this outfit, this outfit for fucktards, this outfit for fucktards that a twenty-year-old has ordered me to wear, then I am admitting that he is in charge and I am a fucktard. I didn't even know what a fucktard was but I knew I would feel pathetic if I submitted to this child-bully's demands and so, with no one paying any attention to me any more, I hung up the King Wolf costume, turned around and left the party.

I don't know if you've ever left a party early because you think everyone there is an arsehole, let alone not even entered a party for the same reason, but it's one of the best feelings a human being can experience. I can't recommend it highly enough. As I walked away I remember thinking to myself, *I should do this every time. Every time I go to a party I should just look around and if I don't like the look of the people in the room I should turn around and go home. Or if I choose to stay I should leave as soon as anyone says something rude to me.* This is how I would live my life from now on. I felt so alive, and on Halloween – the night of the dead!

I didn't need that King Wolf costume; I already felt like the King Wolf because this is the kind of thing the King Wolf would do, just tell everyone to get stuffed and then split without saying goodbye. I was the true King Wolf, doing my own thing in my Wolf Kingdom. No one tells the King Wolf what to do.

I stepped outside and walked round the corner, still feeling like a million bucks, when I heard a hushed voice say, 'Excuse me!' I looked across the road and there was a lady in a black dress with a white mask on the top of her head, crouching near a wall.

'Do you have any food?' she asked.

To begin with I assumed she was someone who had forgotten

that the correct phrase was 'trick or treat' and was now having to go down a more literal route. But then she pointed up at a nearby garage. 'There's a fox up there,' she said.

It's almost like she knew I was the King Wolf. When you've got problems with foxes it's only common sense to summon the King Wolf to defend you; she was probably very relieved to see the King Wolf whilst she was in this particular predicament. I walked over to her.

'Pardon me?' said I, the Wolf King.

'What do foxes eat?' she asked. 'Bread?'

I thought about it for a second. 'Maybe cat food?'

She took this news very badly. 'Oh of course it's cat food, how could I be so stupid?!' she scolded herself. 'Why would I think foxes liked bread?!?!'

'Don't be hard on yourself,' I said (because I wasn't even sure that they liked cat food, to be honest) and then, out of nowhere, a fox appeared on top of the garage, staring down at both of us with a calm confidence. As the fox and I stared at each other it occurred to me that maybe foxes and wolves were on the same side. I certainly felt like there was a mutual respect between us. Something about the way he held my gaze told me that we were equals. Maybe this was the King Fox, who's to say?

The three of us stood there for twenty minutes. We stared at the fox and it stared back, we chatted to each other about our evenings, I told her about how awful the party had been, all the while the fox looking at us from the garage.

'Where is this party?' she said.

'Just around the corner.' I pointed in the general direction.

'Do you think they have cat food?'

I am sorry to say that I refused to go back to the party with her to see if they had any cat food and to this day it's one of the things I regret the most in life. My flatmate said there were two things I could've done that night that would've secured an absolute win for me. Number one was returning to the party with a nice lady, barging past the skeleton at the door, opening the fridge, taking anything out of it that a fox might like, then leaving and feeding it all to our new friend the King Fox. And the second one was that when I left originally I should have kept the King Wolf outfit instead of hanging it back up. Then I should've brought it home, put it on and taken a photo of myself sitting on my sofa with a beer, then sent it to the friends whose party I stole it from, including a simple message like 'Happy Halloween'.

But instead I said we really should not return to that horrible party, said goodbye and we never saw each other again. Because she was a ghost and had been dead for five hundred years. And the fox was also a ghost. And everyone at the party was dead. And I am writing this from beyond the grave.

Cabadged

There are certain situations where I know going in that something out of the ordinary might occur and the chances of an awful scrape happening are pretty high.

I was booked to perform at the Cambridge May Ball. The Cambridge May Ball is a terribly extravagant event put on by the students of Cambridge University. They all dress in gowns and tuxes, eat tons of food, drink even more than they eat, and plenty of bands, DJs and even comedians come and perform for them. This event seems insane to people who went to other universities, let alone to someone like me who never even went to uni.

Upon arrival I was immediately ushered into a dorm and told to stay there until my stage time. I wasn't allowed to enjoy the festivities under any circumstances because all of the students in attendance had paid a lot of money to be there and it wasn't fair if I experienced the same things for free. As I sat in my dorm I knew that something was bound to happen tonight, something unfortunate that I would later talk about on the radio with Josh. But nothing did. I did my set, it went OK (not great, but OK, just in case anyone who was in attendance is reading this book) and I was ushered off the premises. I should also point out that I did the Cambridge May Ball again a couple of years later and it was lovely. The first time I performed I did the Jesus May Ball and the second time I did the St John's May Ball. Jesus wasn't nice but St John's was. Which is confusing because in the Bible, St John learnt from Jesus. The student has become the master, I guess.

It was two a.m. by the time I finished my set and as I couldn't get a train home I had arranged to stay at Cambridge local and one quarter of the Fell Foot Four David Trent's house for the night. David had left a key out for me so I could let myself in and sleep on the fold-out sofa in the living room. When I arrived at David's there was a Post-It note on the front door. Written on it in green biro was 'CABADGE MOMENT!' with a circular green biro scribble underneath it. I presumed it was not intended for me and let myself in. I brushed my teeth as quietly as I could then, in the dark, climbed into bed. The sheets were cold and clammy. They felt almost rubbery. Had David put a rubber sheet down for me? Did he think I'd be getting lashed at the May Ball then arrive at his family home completely blasted and disgrace myself in my sleep? I got up, turned the light on and threw back the covers. What I saw was unexpected and confusing.

A sporting chance

Someone had carefully laid several cabbage leaves across the bed sheets. There was a napkin in the center of the leaves; I picked it up and read it. 'You got Cabadged ha ha ha ha ha ha ha ha ha ha ha ha lol lol lol from Mick.'

Mick is David's nine-year-old son. So the Post-It on the front door had been meant for me. I instantly realised that the Post-It had been a genius touch: he had basically told me what was about to happen and it was my fault that I then continued to walk into this trap despite being given a clear heads-up. But I still didn't fully understand what had just occurred and I was exhausted so I wearily picked up all the cabbage leaves, put them in the bin along with the napkin, then went to sleep.

I woke up at nine and had to rush to the train station to catch my train home. When I left David's house it was empty, so I locked the door behind me, posted the key back through the letter box and legged it. Later that day I received a phone call from David.

'What the fuck is your problem?' he barked.

Oh no, I must've done something wrong while at his house. Did I do the wrong thing with the key maybe? Perhaps I had put the bedding in the wrong place once I'd stripped the bed? Did I even strip the bed? I couldn't remember now!

'Mick cabadged you and you didn't even cabadge him back!' Which was the last thing I expected him to say.

'Pardon me, David?'

'He was all excited about what you would do in return and not only did you not do anything, you didn't even acknowledge it! Who gets cabadged and just carries on as though nothing has happened? It's really weird, everyone in my house thinks you're really weird, it's all anyone is talking about is how weird you are!'

'I didn't know I was meant to cabadge him back, what even is cabadging? Is it a thing all the youngsters are doing these days?'

'No, Mick made it up yesterday when he cabadged you and it's not going to become a thing the youngsters are doing because you didn't even cabadge him back like a normal person!'

'How can it be normal if no one's ever done it before?'

'When a child puts cabbage leaves in your bed and leaves you a funny note you acknowledge it, you don't brush it off and get on with your day!'

'I was going to miss my train, I had to rush off, I didn't have time to look for a cabbage!'

'Well you better cabadge him back and make this right!'

'Fine!'

'Fine!'

I did suggest to David that I could wait until Mick's eighteenth birthday and fill his bed with carrots as it'd be the last thing he'd suspect but David pointed out to me that by the time Mick was eighteen he'd be old enough to beat the shit out of me so that plan was swiftly abandoned.

I suppose I was just unaware that when someone pranks you, it is customary to prank them back in return. I now finally understood why my ex-colleague from the kitchen was so pissed off when I got him to help me wash the dessert sauce and fish juice off of my car. He must've expected me to do the same to his car the following day and then we could both delight in being even-stevens. I now felt bad for making such a faux pas all those years ago. If only I'd known, I'd have covered his car in cod batter and filled his petrol tank with milkshake. He'd have loved that.

The day after the cabadging I popped into Josh's radio show and, on air, told Josh, Producer Neil, Intern Charles and guest Zoe Lyons what had happened and asked for suggestions as to how I could cabadge this boy back. The best suggestion came from a listener who said I should send him a PlayStation 4 box full of cabbages so that he gets all excited, believing he has received a PlayStation, then opens the box and cries his eyes out.

'Great idea,' I said on the radio. 'I will do that.'

Unfortunately for me, somewhere in Cambridge the very same nine-year-old I was intending to do this to was listening to the radio with his father, cackling and rubbing his hands together.

A week or so later, I got cabadged again.

I had ordered a book by my favourite author and a DVD by

286 JAMES ACASTER'S CLASSIC SCRAPES

my favourite director online and woke up to an email informing me that they would be delivered today. I had to go out in the morning though and received another email informing me they had tried to deliver my packages but I'd been out and that they'd try again. But when I returned home that afternoon there was a note from the postman on the doormat, one of those 'Sorry we missed you' notes, informing me that my package was waiting for me at the post office and I would need to bring a form of ID in order to collect it.

So the next morning I woke up half an hour earlier than I needed to, grabbed my passport and walked fifteen minutes to the post office, then stood in a queue for half an hour, then proved who I was to the lady at the desk before she then handed me my delivery. But the box was much bigger than I had anticipated. Usually DVDs and books are delivered in a flat package, not a large box about the size of a microwave. I walked out of the post office and immediately opened the box in the street because I was way too curious to wait until I got home.

Inside there was loads of shredded paper, and buried inside the shredded paper was half a cabbage wrapped in clingfilm. There was a note on top of the cabbage that read 'HA HA CABEDGED (AGAIN) MICK' and underneath the message he had drawn a picture of a bicycle with an arrow pointing to it that said 'random bike'.

I had queued up for my own cabadging. Or was it cabedging? I didn't know any more. It'd happened to me twice and been spelt different both times, I assume to mess with me even further, and it'd worked. He was in my head now to the point where I didn't even know what the proper, Oxford English Dictionary spelling of cabbage was either. Not only that but I had proved who I was with my own passport in order to be cabedged. And why was half a cabbage somehow more unsettling than a whole cabbage? I didn't know but it was. I felt most unsettled. The 'random bike' was a real psychological backhander from the boy as well. I wasn't trying to work out what it meant, it's just that he was flaunting his happiness in my face, that while I'm getting cabadged he's chilling out drawing bicycles for fun and loving it. He had heard my chat on Josh's radio show, heard about my plan to send him cabbages in a PlayStation box and had decided to strike before I had the chance and now *I* had fallen for the very trick I was supposed to be getting *him* with. What's more, he had definitely fluked part of it: he got so lucky that the goodies I had ordered for myself were meant to be delivered on the exact same day and that I'd got an email telling me they'd tried to deliver them but I was out. What are the chances?! The very last thing I was suspecting was a cabadging when I went to that post office. It was far too coincidental. But it worked out wonderfully for Mick: I was so excited to receive my DVD and book and all I got was cabadged. If I was to get revenge now it'd have to be even better than this cabedging and the first cabadging combined. Add to that the fact that the more I get cabadged and don't retaliate, the weirder people will think I am, and you really start to get an idea of the urgency of the situation. I must not be defeated and I must not be made to look like a weirdo by a nine-year-old boy.

A fortnight later and my father and I were lucky enough to see the Monty Python reunion show at the O2 together. We had arranged to go with David Trent and his father. And as soon as I arrived at the O2 David's dad cabadged me. He was holding a plastic bag and smiling.

'I've brought you a present,' he smirked, and as soon as I saw his twinkling eyes I knew what was about to happen. He reached into the bag and handed me a beautifully wrapped half-sphere, with colourful wrapping paper and a lovely bow tied around it and, lo and behold, when I unwrapped it, it was another half a cabbage wrapped in clingfilm. (Was it the other half of the half a cabbage I'd received in the post? I'll never know because I'd already thrown it in the bin.) He'd even written a note informing me that I'd been cabadged and spelt cabadged the same way Mick had done. He was chuckling so much when I opened it.

Cabadging had become inter-generational and that was the last thing I needed. Plus this had been the first time I'd been cabadged face to face, when the cabadger could see my reaction and revel in my frustration at having half a cabbage to carry around with me all night at the O2. I looked like a hardcore Monty Python fan carrying half a cabbage around as a reference to a Python sketch nobody's even heard of. Sitting in the audience waiting until they did my favourite 'Half a cabbage' sketch so I could throw my half a cabbage on stage and win the respect of Cleese et al forever. Instead I left with no respect from anyone, not even from myself and certainly not from et al.

From then on the cabadging was relentless and could happen at any time, in any place and there was no telling who the cabadger would be. It became a big, unwelcome part of my life.

My girlfriend at the time lived in New Zealand, and sent me a cabbage she had made out of clay. She sent me that in the post. She had to make it herself and then pay for it to be sent to me.

Audience members sent cabbages backstage for me. One person sent a bag of cabbage seeds; another delivered a branch of Brussels sprouts with a gift tag attached to the end that read 'mini cabadged'; someone made a chocolate cake that did not contain cabbage but looked exactly like a cabbage. (They had made it by painting a cabbage with chocolate, allowing it to set then peeling the chocolate off of the leaves before rebuilding the chocolate cabbage around a cake. This one was actually quite nice.)

Someone had started a Cabadging twitter account and was regularly tweeting me images of cabbages. The first was a picture of a cabbage with the words 'Oi oi Savoy' written underneath it and the second was a picture of a van full of cabbages saying 'special delivery for Mr Acastor.'

During the final week of the Edinburgh festival I received a letter in the post (which is pretty rare for a house you're only living in for a month, so I should've already been suspicious). I opened it, thinking maybe it'd be something nice from my parents, perhaps a letter telling me how proud of me they were, but no, it was the wettest, limpest cabbage leaf I'd received so far, complete with another note from Mick taunting me about getting cabadged. I was beside myself. I suddenly longed for the days when I spent the Edinburgh Festival in a flooded tent, at least then people couldn't send me goddamn leaves in the post. But the handwriting on the front of the envelope didn't match the handwriting on the cabadge note. Plus I was living with David Trent, Mick's father, and it would make no sense for him to post me a letter when he could've just left it on my bed. I knew I recognised the handwriting from somewhere, but where? Then

David Trent walked in and asked, 'Did you get the cabbage leaf that Josh sent you?' JOSH?!

Josh Widdicombe himself had sent me a single wilted cabbage leaf in the post, letting me know that I could now trust absolutely no one. Until then he had been my confidant, counselling me through this whole ordeal, but even he was cabadging me now. It's like if you went to see your psychiatrist and they said, 'Yeah, I've been sleeping with your wife.'

One day Josh and I phoned Mick live on air so I could give him a piece of my mind and put the fear in him a little bit. I told him how I would have my revenge, how he was going to get what's coming to him and that he'd rue the day he ever crossed me. When Josh (the treacherous little toad) asked Mick how this made him feel there was a pause at the other end of the line and then Mick said, very calmly and very plainly, 'I don't feel anything.'

Who the hell was I up against?! It was like talking to a serial killer remorseless on death row, not regretting his past transgressions and with no fear of what was to come. I couldn't see his face because it was a call, but I would wager he didn't blink once during the entire conversation. I started to plot and plan. He might feel nothing now but soon he *will* feel sorry he ever messed with James Acaster.

I had to cabadge him back for several reasons. Revenge, pride, dignity. But I also needed to cabadge him because I felt like it was actually important on a higher level. In the past I had often failed when it came to following through on pointless challenges. I had given up when collecting the Giant Yellow W's of

Northamptonshire; I had only managed five out of seven days when trying to fill a week with new experiences as a teenager. If I didn't cabadge this no-good punk kid then the whole cabadging thing would become yet another pointless event that briefly consumed my life but failed to deliver anything resembling a payoff – just a waste of time for all concerned. And this would be even worse because it had been made public; people knew about it and were invested in it. If I let this peter out then I won't be the only one feeling deflated – I'll have let down the listeners of the Josh Widdicombe show.

24 September 2014

Today was the day. I had a tour show in Cambridge and nothing planned beforehand and so I caught a train that would get me into Cambridge station just after noon, giving me plenty of time to cabadge Mick Trent.

I had liaised with his mother, Polly, since I knew his father could not be trusted. To be frank, I wasn't 100 per cent certain Polly could be trusted and there was every chance that I was putting in a lot of effort just to be greeted at the door with a tub of coleslaw by the boy's laughing mother (at this point it was the only form of cabbage I'd not had my life ruined by), but she was the only member of the family who hadn't cabadged me yet so it was a risk I had to take. Before I got to the house I had to buy some cabbages. Plural, of course. I had been cabadged countless times by this point, so there was no way a single cabbage was going to even the score. My plan was simple: I was going to replace every single item in Mick's bedroom with a cabbage.

292 JAMES ACASTER'S CLASSIC SCRAPES

Take. That.

As soon as I got off the train I headed to the nearest supermarket but was surprised to discover there were no cabbages on the shelves. I went to the supermarket over the road to find they had also sold out of cabbages. By the time the second supermarket had no cabbages to speak of, I started to get paranoid. *He's bought them all*, I thought to myself. *Mick Trent has purchased every single cabbage in Cambridge and he's gearing up for one big mammoth attack. Oh God. I'm on his turf! What was I thinking? I'm wandering round his hometown and I'm completely unarmed. He knows these streets! He OWNS these streets maybe?*

The third supermarket had some cabbages on sale but not enough. I bought them all anyway then flagged down a taxi and asked it to take me to Mick's address but to stop at every supermarket along the way. We stopped at about five supermarkets and three of them sold cabbages. Every time I went inside, the cabbie would keep the meter running. (Some people have asked why I didn't just hire a car for the day but given my driving history I don't think that's a good idea. It'd be the worst way to go, to write off a hire car full of cabbages, cabadging myself to death in the process.) By the time I got to Mick's house I had about twenty cabbages and very little money.

Polly let me into the house and I set about moving all of Mick's belongings out of his bedroom and into his parents' bedroom. And then I started to arrange the cabbages. It very quickly became apparent that I had underestimated the amount of possessions a nine-year-old could possess. Twenty cabbages dotted around a tidy bedroom looked pretty rubbish. And so

I called a cab and went to a bigger supermarket and bought *twenty-five more cabbages*. Then I returned to the boy's house and filled his room with the new cabbages, along with some Brussel sprouts scattered between the cabbages for good measure, filling in all the gaps. I made sure the cabbages were varied as well – red, white, savoy, green. It actually looked rather beautiful.

There was a point where I started to wonder who the joke was really on here. I had spent all day cabadging Mick. I was twenty-nine years old. I had been running around all over Cambridge buying cabbages. The cost of the cabbages combined with the train and cab fare came to over £150. I'm meant to be an adult. The whole thing was oddly stressful and, in many ways, the worst day of my life.

With his room all set and his mother collecting him from school I wrote CABADGE MOMENT on a Post-It and stuck it to the door, a green scribble beneath the message, to give him the same sporting chance he had given me. I then scampered off to the bathroom and locked the door, hiding in there and listening with great anticipation.

I heard the front door open and the sound of Mick denying any knowledge of what the Post-It note was about to his mum. Polly had knocked it out of the park; she was immediately blaming Mick for the Post-It, thus confusing him even more. I then heard, 'What the hell is all my stuff doing in your bedroom?!?!?' Perfect! He had noticed his stuff had been moved before even going into his own room; this was playing out beautifully. Polly continued to play a blinder by accusing Mick of moving his stuff into her bedroom without asking. He was adamant he had done no such thing; I could hear his voice crack a little as he got more frustrated. Lovely, lovely, lovely stuff.

But as I heard him open the door to his bedroom I found myself thinking, *I really hope he doesn't cry*. It was the first time that thought had entered my mind all day. Until then I'd been riding on pure adrenalin and not stopped to consider the possibility that I may have gone too far.

Standing in that bathroom I started to see everything from an outsider's perspective. A nine-year-old child had sent me a couple of cabbages and I had retaliated by spending £150 on filling his bedroom with cabbages and was currently hiding in his house so that I could leap out and rub his face in it when the time came. This was an awful idea. Mick would probably have nightmares about cabbages for the rest of his life. I was probably about to put this kid through a lifetime of therapy. On the bright side, if that did happen, I would definitely have won.

Then I heard Mick shout, 'What?!?!' at the top of his voice and my whole body tensed. I knew I had to fully commit to this now, regardless of his reaction, so I swiftly tiptoed out of my hiding place, ran into his bedroom, pointed in his face and declared, 'CABADGED! You got cabadged mate, look at them! Look at all the cabbages! Count them if you like! You. Got. Cabadged!'

I should point out that, regardless of how it comes across on the page, I actually didn't go as big as I could've when rubbing it in his face because I was so worried about hurting his feelings. If he ended up properly upset I didn't want to be halfway through taunting him as the tears began to roll. But he didn't cry. In true Mick Trent fashion, he didn't feel anything. He shrugged, picked up his tennis racket, and then proceeded to hit Brussel sprouts at me with the racket while I cowered on the bed. I hate Mick Trent.

*

Mick's reaction was irrelevant though. At this point the only thing that mattered was following through on something stupid for once, and I had done it. I'd failed to do A Week Of New Things and I'd failed at The Great W Challenge but I'd triumphantly cabadged a primary school kid like a total boss. I should've celebrated by spending the evening at the nearest karaoke bar and singing 'Every Little Thing She Does Is Magic' by The Police to a room full of strangers, maybe even changing the lyrics to 'Every little thing she does is *Cabbage*', then getting a cab (probably using the same driver I'd had for the cabadging that day) all the way to Kettering, unlocking my friend's old garage and setting the W's free, flinging them into the wild (the street), continuing to sing 'Every Little Thing She Does Is Cabbage', maybe incorporating it into a medley of some sort – 'Every Little Thing She Does Is Cabbage' into 'La La La Humpty' into 'Woodcutter's Prayer'. I didn't feel like I'd won but I felt like I'd achieved something, or *not* achieved something – and that was the whole point maybe, I wasn't sure. All I knew was that a huge weight had been lifted from my shoulders (and my wallet). I felt terrific. *This is how Dave Gorman must feel all the time*, I thought.

At this point some of you may be worried that after the cabadging had taken place, fifty perfectly good cabbages got thrown in the bin, but don't fret. As I said, I had a gig that night, and I ended the show by handing out fifty cabbages to members of the audience as they left. What I learnt from this is that people love red cabbage infinitely more than they love any other type of cabbage. There was no contest – people were fighting over the red ones and couldn't care less about the others. It was a real eye opener. I have since learned that red cabbage contains ten times more Vitamin A and twice the amount of iron than a green cabbage so I guess that explains it. People bloody love Vitamin A.

Eventually Mick admitted that I had done a pretty good cabadging and a truce was called. I am pleased to report he has not cabadged me since. A man of his word, he has honoured our agreement and good on him. I too have honoured the truce, although that's not hard because I have no desire to get tormented by any variety of veg ever again. And for the most part, the general public have stopped cabadging me also – those with any respect for the rules have anyway. They have not stopped cabadging each other, though. Mick accidentally started a craze and it's one that has been damaging people's relationships for a good few years now. The rules are simple – cabadge someone, then don't stop cabadging that someone until they cabadge you back. You can cabadge them in any way you like but once they have cabadged you back you are not permitted to cabadge them again, unless of course they cabadge you and in doing so trigger a whole new round of cabadging. Congratulations, Mick, what a legacy.

My greatest achievement

Farewell

Farewell

At the start of the book I said that if you compare the first story to the final story you'll see that they essentially happen to the same person, a person who has learned nothing throughout his entire life. And that's more or less true. There's no lesson at the end of all these mistakes, I'm afraid. The lesson was going to be 'don't do any of the stuff I did', but I doubt you were planning on doing that anyway.

While writing up all the scrapes I did realise that the reason these things seem to happen to me more than the average person is because I tend to go along with things instead of approaching anything with caution, so I guess the only lesson of the book is this: do not be open to new experiences, avoid anything that could potentially not work out for you, and enter into everything with the utmost suspicion. Never 'let yourself go', do not trust anybody and never ever put yourself out there (emotionally or physically). What I'm saying is, don't take any risks and you'll be fine.

Cool.

Oh, and you shouldn't let yourself into someone's house and take a crap in their downstairs toilet without their knowledge or permission either.

Oddly, since telling these stories on Josh's show I hardly ever get into any scrapes any more. I've no idea why this is. Maybe because I'm older and have my wits about me a little bit more, or maybe talking about all these scrapes on the show every week was actually a form of therapy I didn't even realise I was taking part in. Maybe through explaining and analysing all of these past events I've cured myself somehow and am now a stable and sensible human being. Or maybe I am just less open than I used to be. Maybe once a person gets past thirty they don't say yes to everything, hoping something amazing will happen; we just assume it won't and don't roll the dice as often. When put like that it's kind of depressing. Also, I just called myself 'stable and sensible' which is a lie and one that I will get called out on by the friends and family who will read this book (after all, they may be the only people who do).

I can't say I miss those days but, like a lot of people, I look back on my past misfortunes fondly. No matter how bad something was the first time around, I love reminiscing about it as if those were the golden days. If I walked past that bush in Basingstoke today I'd stop and look at it wistfully, remembering that night as though it were my own wedding day when in actual fact it was a waking nightmare and there's no way I would want to go through it ever again. It's very easy to idealise a more innocent time in your life. That time when you were more naïve, more optimistic. I think these are the main two ingredients needed when getting into scrapes – naïvety and optimism. As long as you have those two things there will be no end to the binds you'll get yourself into.

Obviously, I'll surely experience more scrapes as time goes on but it strikes me as a little curious that none have taken place since the show ended. What will most likely happen is that the day this book comes out, an almighty scrape will befall me and it'll sting doubly hard because I could've put it in the book if it had just happened a couple of months earlier. I would then have to go around deliberately trying to get into scrapes in order to accrue enough tales to fill a second book. Although I sincerely hope there is no second book; I just want to have a nice life. Please, God.

And so, I *hope* this is goodbye. As far as such stories go, at least. Thank you for reading my book and thank you to those of you who listened to us when we did the radio show too.

And if you're the kind of person who gets into a lot of scrapes then my thoughts are with you: may the universe guide you and catch you every time you fall, may your friends learn from your mistakes, and may all bystanders laugh at them. But with each and every scrape may you grow stronger, smarter and more resilient. May you see humour in your own downfall and silver linings in every cloud, albeit clouds that you yourself have created, like mushroom clouds as opposed to cumulus clouds and other nice types of cloud. Some people are lucky: they grasp the world immediately, they understand how everything works and appear to breeze through each day without a care in the world. But others have to learn the hard way and at the end of the day, maybe they turn out to be the wisest of them all. For they not only understand how to live life but they also understand how not to live life. Failure cannot be understood in theory, only in practice, sometimes over and over and over again. Only when one has experienced both sides of the coin can one understand the true value of that coin. Yes, if you only look at the side of the coin that says the value *on* it then maybe you can say the value is 10p or what have you but it's not the same as looking at both sides and absorbing all the information, the details, the pattern (there's probably a nice drawing on the other side that you wouldn't have seen if you'd just stayed on the side with the value written on it, for example); only then can you completely *understand* as opposed to just *knowing* how much the coin is really worth, and the same applies to bank notes also. I once saw a poster in an office that read, 'Your best teacher is your last mistake' and it filled me with pride. I may not have gone to university but my god, have I been educated. My professors were a skydiving instructor, a French porcelain salesman, a nobhead named Alistair and a nine-year-old boy with unlimited access to cabbages. They are the ones who set *my* exams. And yes I failed those exams but in failing them I actually passed them because that's the way you pass an exam about mistakes – you fail. And all the people who 'pass' the exam are the ones who actually fail the exam in the end. But in doing so maybe they also end up passing them because they failed. I don't work on an exam board; maybe everyone passes because everyone fails. And isn't that what life is all about? We are all failures and as such we are roaring successes. Each and every one of us.

When I was a baby I urinated into my own mouth. Thirty-two years on, I regret nothing.

Except crashing all those cars.